Destiny by Design

A SERMON IN POETRY

Yvonne Rivers

YVONNE RIVERS

Copyright © 2016 Yvonne Rivers.

All rights reserved. No part of this book may be used or reproduced by any means, graphic, electronic, or mechanical, including photocopying, recording, taping or by any information storage retrieval system without the written permission of the author except in the case of brief quotations embodied in critical articles and reviews.

Scripture quotations taken from the Amplified® Bible (AMP), Copyright © 2015 by The Lockman Foundation Used by permission. www.Lockman.org

WestBow Press books may be ordered through booksellers or by contacting:

WestBow Press
A Division of Thomas Nelson & Zondervan
1663 Liberty Drive
Bloomington, IN 47403
www.westbowpress.com
1 (866) 928-1240

Because of the dynamic nature of the Internet, any web addresses or links contained in this book may have changed since publication and may no longer be valid. The views expressed in this work are solely those of the author and do not necessarily reflect the views of the publisher, and the publisher hereby disclaims any responsibility for them.

Any people depicted in stock imagery provided by Thinkstock are models, and such images are being used for illustrative purposes only. Certain stock imagery © Thinkstock.

ISBN: 978-1-5127-6830-5 (sc)
ISBN: 978-1-5127-6832-9 (hc)
ISBN: 978-1-5127-6831-2 (e)

Library of Congress Control Number: 2016920739

Print information available on the last page.

WestBow Press rev. date: 02/28/2017

Contents

Acknowledgments xi
Prelude xiii

Alignment in Christ 1
Arise and Shine 2
Army of God 3
Assigned to Fulfill Destiny 4
Attitude of Gratitude 5
Behold Him 6
Be Not Afraid 7
Because 8
Before Time 9
Bless My Home 10
Blessing Beyond Measure 11
Blind Faith 12
Bone of My Bone 13
Brilliance 14
Called to Excellence 15
Chains Are Breaking 16
Choices 17
Cross Over 18
Dare to Dream 19
Daughters of Destiny and Purpose 20
Delay Is Not Denied 21
Don't Mourn for Me 22

Dreams	23
Encourage Yourself in the Lord	24
Expand Your Wings	25
Abide in the Vine	26
Amazing Grace	27
Anointed to Prosper	28
Expectant Faith	29
Failure Is Not an Option	30
Favor	31
Favor of God	32
Finish Your Course	33
Free	34
Freedom Has a Voice	35
Fruit of the Spirit: Heaven's Grocery Store	36
God's Timing	38
God's Visionary	39
He Arose	40
Heroes of Faith	41
Glory of the Lord	42
Empowered to Prosper	43
Encounter of the God Kind	44
I Be Free	45
I Am Woman	46
Harvest Time	47
Healed, Delivered, and Whole	48
It Is Time	49
He Touched Me	50
It's Not About You	51
Journey of Life	52
Justified	53
Kingdom Movement	54
Lead Me	55

Contents

Acknowledgments xi
Prelude xiii

Alignment in Christ 1
Arise and Shine 2
Army of God 3
Assigned to Fulfill Destiny 4
Attitude of Gratitude 5
Behold Him 6
Be Not Afraid 7
Because 8
Before Time 9
Bless My Home 10
Blessing Beyond Measure 11
Blind Faith 12
Bone of My Bone 13
Brilliance 14
Called to Excellence 15
Chains Are Breaking 16
Choices 17
Cross Over 18
Dare to Dream 19
Daughters of Destiny and Purpose 20
Delay Is Not Denied 21
Don't Mourn for Me 22

Dreams	23
Encourage Yourself in the Lord	24
Expand Your Wings	25
Abide in the Vine	26
Amazing Grace	27
Anointed to Prosper	28
Expectant Faith	29
Failure Is Not an Option	30
Favor	31
Favor of God	32
Finish Your Course	33
Free	34
Freedom Has a Voice	35
Fruit of the Spirit: Heaven's Grocery Store	36
God's Timing	38
God's Visionary	39
He Arose	40
Heroes of Faith	41
Glory of the Lord	42
Empowered to Prosper	43
Encounter of the God Kind	44
I Be Free	45
I Am Woman	46
Harvest Time	47
Healed, Delivered, and Whole	48
It Is Time	49
He Touched Me	50
It's Not About You	51
Journey of Life	52
Justified	53
Kingdom Movement	54
Lead Me	55

Love Is	56
Man of Valor	57
Matter of the Heart	58
Mission Possible	60
Mommy Dearest	61
Mother's Love	62
Mother, Grandmother, and Servant	63
My Authentic Self	64
Run Toward Your Destiny	66
Set Time	67
Spirit of the Lord	68
Stand Your Ground	69
Stay in Your Lane	70
Stop the Violence	71
Strength for the Journey	72
Success	73
Sufficient Grace	74
Surrender All	75
Survivor	76
Thankful Heart	77
The Best Is Yet to Come	78
The Blessing	79
The Force of Faith	80
The Gift	81
The Struggle Is Over	82
Time of Restoration	83
Tribute to Mother	84
True Friendship	85
Turn It Around	87
Unto Us	88
Victorious	89
Victorious Fight	90

What Is a Father?	91
What Is Love?	92
Who Am I?	93
Wisdom	94
You Came	95
My Precious	96
Name So Sweet	97
No More Tears	98
No Scars	99
Open Doors	100
My Refuge	101
Past, Present, and Future	102
Peace	103
Prayer of Faith	104
Price of Freedom	106
Priceless	107
Rejoice This Day	108
Rise Up in Faith	109
I Dream	110
Hiding Place	111
Power of Praise	112
My Healer	113
Women of Grace	114
My Child	115
Make a Comeback	116
Masterpiece	117
In the Valley	118
Image	119
I Exalt Thee	120
Message with a Mission	121
I Cry	122
I Am Whole	123

Power of Worship and Praise	124
Rise Up	125
Relentless Praise	127
Season of Increase	128
Season of Favor	130
Season of Life	131
Season of Prayer	133
The God of More Than Enough	134
Blessings of Increase	135
Set the Captives Free	136
Stand Firm	137
Greatness	138
God of Many Chances	139
God Is Able	140
God Is	141
Fruitful Harvest	142
Walk Out Your Dreams	143
Willing Vessel	144
Faithful God	145
Expanding Wings to Fly	146
Excellence	147
Write the Vision	148
Tribute to a Friend	149
The Woman at the Well	150
Encounter of the God Kind	151
You Reign	152
The Overflow Blessing	153
Let Down Your Net	154
Pregnant with Expectancy	155
Bountiful Harvest	156
I Get Up	157

Acknowledgments

I thank God for giving me the gift of writing poetry.

I thank my wonderful husband, Arthur, for supporting me in all my endeavors.

I also give thanks to my pastors, Bishop Steven and Dr. Marlene Williams, at Lord of the Harvest C.F.C., and to my church family.

My love goes out to my children: Damon (Anita), Terrell, Shana, and Justin; and to my grandchildren: Ashley, Chasity, Krez, and Makayla.

I am thankful for all my family and friends who have supported me. I am grateful for all their support, prayers, and encouraging words.

I would like to thank Eric Jones with Visions Digital Image for my photo on the back cover of my book. I would like to thank Joe Mueller for the beautiful picture on the cover of my book and my son Damon for the design of the book cover.

Prelude

Yvonne has been writing poetry over 25 years. She started writing cards for birthdays and other special occasions. Yvonne's co-workers were touched by the cards made especially for them.

A dear friend put Yvonne in touch with a local company that made greeting cards. They said that her work was not good enough. That statement did not discourage her, Yvonne kept on writing and blessing others. Yvonne's response is, "Don't let anyone deter you from your destiny".

Alignment in Christ

There is a shift in the atmosphere;
Change is in the air.
Arise and shine, for thy light has come.
We are moving toward our assignments.
We have marching orders.
We are ready and able.
We are suited with our armor.
The battle is not ours; it is the Lord's.
Satan comes to kill, steal, and destroy.
God has come to give us life, and life more abundantly.
Generals are rising up to lead the kingdom of God.
God's word is powerful, sharper than any two-edged sword.
We have on the whole armor of God.
We have our loins girded about with truth.
We will not be defeated; we walk by faith and not by sight.
We have the breastplate of righteousness.
Our feet are shod with the gospel of peace.
We have the shield of faith and the helmet of salvation.
We have the sword of the Spirit.
We are strong and mighty in God.
We pull down every stronghold.
We bring them into subjugation to the Word of God.
Every knee must bow; every tongue must confess
that Jesus Christ is Lord.
We are not here to take sides; we are here to take over.
We are anointed, appointed, aligned, and on assignment.
We will not be delayed, denied, deceived, or deterred.
We are ready, able, and in alignment to conquer all.

Arise and Shine

Arise and shine, for thy light has come.
The glory of the Lord has risen upon you.
God will turn your sadness into praise.
Your mourning will turn into gladness.
Your crying will turn into laughter.
Your trials will turn into testimony.
Your mess will turn into message.
God is good, and his mercy endures forever.
God's grace is sufficient for you.
You will triumph over every obstacle.
You will jump over every wall.
You will praise the Lord, your God.
Give God praise through every situation.
Dust yourself off, and speak the Word of God.
Rejoice in the Lord, and be of good courage.
The Word of God is a mighty weapon.
The Word of God sends out an ambush.
The Word will accomplish your destiny.
Take territory for the kingdom of God.
Greatness is upon you; walk in the Spirit.
Do not walk in the flesh.
Arise and shine, for thy light has come.

Army of God

We are the army of God.
We are well able and equipped.
We are strong and mighty.
We are more than a conqueror.
We win every battle.
Jesus Christ is our commander in chief.
The Holy Spirit gives us inside information.
We battle not against flesh and blood.
We battle against spiritual wickedness.
We seek the Lord, and He directs our paths.
We have on the whole armor of God.
We have our loins girded with truth.
We have the breastplate of righteousness.
Our feet are shod with the gospel of peace.
We have the shield of faith,
by which we quench all the fiery darts of the wicked one.
We have the helmet of salvation and the sword of the Spirit,
which is the Word of God.
We pray in the Spirit, with all kinds of prayers and requests.
We are alert and ready to do battle.

Assigned to Fulfill Destiny

I was formed, fitted, and fashioned to fulfill destiny.
I was designed to make a mark in this century.
I was created, craved, and called to be a blessing.
My voice is one crying out in the wilderness that the lost will come to Jesus Christ.
My eyes see in the realm of the Spirit.
Impossibilities are possible.
Shortcomings are transformed into uprisings.
Experiences in the valley become victorious encounters.
Lack becomes abundance in every area.
Inabilities become opportunities to excel.
Doubts become overcoming circumstances.
Disappointments turn into triumphs.
Failures become successes above measure.
I will not settle, stop, or retreat on my assignment.
Many are called, but few are chosen.
I will walk out every area that my Father has called me to do.
My ears are open to hear what the Spirit of God is saying.
My hands are busy with productive things.
My heart is filled with God's love for people.
I reach out to help and not hinder.
My arms embrace with comfort and love.
My feet are on the path that was chosen for me.
My mouth speaks blessings and not curses.
My mind is renewed daily with the Word of God.
I declare and decree the doors of opportunities are open now.
Favor covers me like a cloud.
Goodness and mercy follow me.
I am empowered to conquer, compete, and complete every assignment designed for me in Jesus's name.
Amen.

Attitude of Gratitude

I have an attitude of gratitude.
God has blessed me beyond my wildest dreams.
Whenever I think something is impossible,
God said his promises are yes and amen.
God's word is true and forever settled in heaven.
I praise God for what he has done, what he is doing, and what He will do in my life.
Our heavenly Father is so loving and generous.
He wants his children to prosper and to be in good health, even as our souls prosper.
Prosper means to be blessed in every area of our lives.
Whatever we put our hands to do is blessed.
God is good, and his mercy endures forever.
He desires that we have no lack but live in abundance.
God wants us blessed, to be a blessing to others.
God is our strong tower; he is our source.
God is everything to us; he is our all in all.
He is everything, from the beginning to the end.
Trust in the Lord with all your heart and lean not to your own understanding.
Let the Lord lead and direct your path.
God will never lead you astray.
Give God praises, and have a thankful heart.
Your attitude will determine your altitude.

Behold Him

Behold the King of glory,
who is the Lord, mighty in battle.
Behold the King of glory,
Lord of Lords, and King of Kings.
Behold the King of glory,
just and true in all his ways.
Behold the King of glory,
He sits high and looks low.
Behold the King of glory,
clothed in righteousness and honor.
Behold the King of glory.
He never sleeps or slumbers.
Behold the King of glory,
His mercy endures forever and ever.
Behold the King of glory,
to Him who does great wonders.
Behold the King of glory,
to Him who made the heavens and the earth.
Behold the King of glory,
who made the sun to rule by day and the moon
to rule at night.
Behold the King of glory,
who sits on the throne and rules forever and ever.
Amen.

Be Not Afraid

Be not afraid or dismayed, saith the Lord.
God has given you power and authority over the enemy.
You have the whole armor.
You have victory over the wiles of the devil.
Jesus has the keys of hell and death.
You are more than a conqueror in Jesus's name.
Fight the good fight of faith; don't faint.
Do not fear, for you have the power of
love and a sound mind.
The Word of God is powerful, sharper than any two-edged sword.
Lean not on your own understanding.
This fight is a spiritual fight, not a natural fight of the flesh.
This fight requires your weapon of prayer against the enemy.
Your prayers will sound the alarm in the heavenlies.
The angelic host responds to the battle cry of prayer
from God's children.
You will pursue, overtake, and recover all.
You will not back up, back down, or bow down to the devil.
The devil is under your feet to tread upon.
Your weapon is mighty in battle through God.
You do not have the spirit of fear.
Having done all to stand, I say, stand therefore; saith
the Lord of Hosts.

Because

Because Jesus died, we can live victoriously.
Because he died, we are healed.
Because he died, we are free.
Because he died, we have liberty.
Because he died, we have peace.
Because of Jesus, we are free from sickness, death, and pain.
Because Jesus lives, we live abundantly.
Because Jesus lives, we are free, and free indeed,
Because Jesus arose, we arise from poverty and sin.
Because Jesus lives, we are more than conquerors.
Because Jesus overcame, we are overcomers with our testimonies.
Because Jesus lives, we are sons and daughters of the kingdom.
Because Jesus lives, we are covered with the blood of the Lamb.
Because Jesus lives, we are sanctified, justified, and glorified.
Because Jesus lives, we are redeemed from the curse of the law.
Because Jesus lives, we rule and reign with him.
Because Jesus lives, we have joy unspeakable and full of glory.

Before Time

God existed before time; He is the I am God.
He called time into being; He is the Alpha and the Omega.
He was in time when there was no time.
He is the first and the last.
He was before the world was formed; He is the beginning and the end.
The earth was void, no form.
He spoke the world into existence.
God said, and it was so; He is the Creator of the heavens and the earth.
God said, and it was so; the earth was formed by the power of the Word.
God spoke, and the land was separated from the sea.
God spoke the planets into the heavenlies.
God saw that everything was good.
God thought and said, "Let us make man in our likeness and our image."
He created man from the dust of the earth, and man was formed.
God blew the breath of life into his nostrils, and man became a living creature.
Then God created the animals, and man named each and every one of them.
Then God said, "It is not good for man to be alone."
God created woman, and her name was Eve; she came from Adam's rib.
God gave man and woman dominion over the earth.

Bless My Home

Lord, bless my home, both night and day.
Bless my home as I go about my way.
Lord, have your angels surround my house.
Watch over me, my children, and my spouse
as we go about our daily route.
Father, I give thanks to you, each and every day.
For without you, I would never be blessed this way.
I am so thankful and blessed.
Lord, only you knew what was best.
So as we go to sleep each night,
we awaken, knowing each day will be bright.
I willl praise you all the days of my life
For giving me a home so beautiful on this site.

Blessing Beyond Measure

What a blessing to see.
What a blessing to be.
What a blessing to hear.
What a blessing to live.
What a blessing to give.
What a blessing to pray.
What a blessing to say.
What a blessing to praise.
What a blessing to lift up holy hands.
What a blessing to sing.
What a blessing to become a hundred years old.
What a blessing to be a soldier so bold.
What a blessing to be whole again.
What a blessing to praise God's holy name.
What a blessing to be a child of the Lord.
What a blessing to be a carrier of the Word as a sword.
What a blessing to give God glory, blessing His holy name.
What a blessing to be God's child, sanctified, blood washed, and born again.

In honor of Pauline Felder

Blind Faith

Blind faith is believing God's word.
Walking by faith and not by sight.
Trusting that God is faithful and true to His word.
Stepping out in faith; knowing His promises are true
and will never fail.
Blind faith is trusting God's hand when you can not
see your way through the storms of life.
Knowing that He will never leave you nor forsake you.
Believing that God is Alpha and Omega; the first and the last.
Trusting that the Word of God is true, from Genesis
to Revelation.
Knowing that you are the apple of His eye and you are His beloved.
Trusting in the Lord and leaning not unto your own understanding.
Blind faith is believing God's word is true and
forever settled in heaven.

Bone of My Bone

You are bone of my bone and flesh of my flesh;
You were made for me and I was made for you.
We entered into a covenant before God and man;
Our years of marriage have helped us to grow stronger together;
We become one, and no man may put us asunder.
God has joined us together in holy matrimony;
I will abide with you with loving-kindness.
Our seed is blessed because we are blessed;
We pray and agree for the blessing of the Lord.
The blessing covers our family, from generation to generation.
Divorce is not an option; we are together until death do us part.
The blessing of the Lord makes us rich and adds no sorrow.
God is the anchor that holds us together.
We have weathered every storm, test, trouble, and disappointment.
The Word of God is our comfort and our refuge.
We run to the Lord, and we are saved.
God has satisfied us with long life.
You are bone of my bone and flesh of my flesh;
We are one.

Brilliance

Brilliance is not just the rock that shines on your finger.
It is the mind of Christ in you, the hope of glory.
It is your thought patterns.
It is how you process information to come to a conclusion.
Brilliance is knowledge of information.
It is how you use what is given to you.
It is time to shift into the next season of greatness.
It is time to do kingdom business in the marketplace.
Brilliance is not just gold, diamonds, and silver.
It is letting God use you in your respective areas.
It is using what you have don't lose it; use it.
It is sharpening your tools for business.
Brilliance is a way of thinking.
It is seeing what others can't see.
It is vision into the supernatural realm.
It is being empowered to prosper, even as your soul prospers.
Brilliance is not all that sparkles and glitters.
It is using your God-given talents and resources.
It is dreaming the impossible dream.
It is daring to go where others won't.
Brilliance is a state of mind.
It is presence, a state of being.
It is knowing that you are here for this appointed time and place.
Brilliance is not just radiance or splendor.
It is a light set upon a hill, God's people doing what they are called to do.
Let your light shine so that men will glorify your Father in heaven.
That is brilliance.

Called to Excellence

I was called out of darkness, into the marvelous light.
I am called to walk in excellence; I have the mind of Christ.
I have gifts, talents, abilities to use in the kingdom of God.
I draw from the well that never runs dry.
The Holy Spirit fills me daily with wise endeavors.
I have an attitude of gratitude; I'm not boastful.
I pray for insight as I go about my daily work.
There is no laziness in me.
My course is set and on track for success.
The Holy Spirit is my comforter; He guides me daily.
God has called His children to rule and reign in this season.
We are leaders, not followers.
Impossibilities become possible.
All things are possible to those who believe.
Every challenge is met with diligence.
I will overtake and conquer every obstacle as I pursue my purpose.
Nothing will delay, destroy, dismantle, or distract my purpose.
I will fulfill my goals, dreams, visions, and destiny in Jesus's name.
Amen.

Chains Are Breaking

The chains are breaking over my life.
The enemy thought he had me, but I got away.
The blood of Jesus covers me daily.
The prayers of the righteous avail much.
I give God the praise for deliverance.
Lack is broken.
Sickness is broken.
Worry is broken.
Self-pity is broken.
Depression is broken.
Doubt is broken.
Bondage is broken.
Negative attitude is broken.
He whom the Son sets free is free indeed.
I'm no longer bound; I'm no longer a victim.
I'm no longer a captive; I'm no longer chained.
I'm free; no more chains holding me.
I'm free to dance; I'm free to praise.
I'm free to lift my hands; I'm free to pray.
I'm free to sing; I'm free to glorify my God.

Choices

The choices we make are so powerful.
Our choices lead us to success or destruction.
God has given us the power to choose.
We have the authority to choose life or death.
We have the power to choose blessings or curses.
Many times our choices are destructive.
We don't realize the effect our choices make.
We are born into sin; so our choices are natural.
We must be born again to make spiritually sound decisions.
Choose this day whom you will serve.
Choose the devil; and lose your life.
Choose Jesus; and regain your life.
God loves us so much, we are given a choice.
We are not made to choose him; the choice is ours.
Father God desires his children to choose life.
Our choices not only affect us, but our family too.
Our choices affect generations to come.
Choose wisely; don't make emotional decisions.
Emotions change like the weather.
Some days sunny, others days cloudy and rainy.
Let the Son shine in your life.
Then you will prosper and have good success.

Cross Over

Just as the slaves crossed over from bondage to the land of the free,
so are we crossing over into 2017.
We are leaving behind disappointment,
discouragement, and delay of dreams.
Now we are forging forward into the New Year.
We press toward the higher calling in Christ Jesus.
We have seen the other side, and we will conquer all
obstacles.
We give God praises for our past, present, and future.
We will trust in the Lord with all our hearts and
lean not on our own understanding.
We inquire of the Holy Spirit for direction.
We are of one accord as we cross over into the New Year.
There is nothing broken, nothing lacking, and nothing missing.
We have one mind, one mouth, one purpose, and we are of one accord.
We will dominate and have dominion over new territory.
We are determined and destined for greatness.
We are on point and on course.
We march toward our goals and dreams.
We have crossed over from darkness into light.
We have been depressed and oppressed, but our God
delivered us out of our mess.
Victory is ours, we will proclaim,
Waving the flag as we obtain the promises of God.
We are appointed, anointed, and assigned to fulfill destiny.
We have purpose, promises, and provision to acquire.
We will spread our wings and take new territory for
the kingdom of God.

Dare to Dream

Dreams are visions waiting to manifest.
Dare to dream big; don't dream small.
Let no one stop your dreams from manifesting.
Look up and never look down.
Press forward, and don't stop.
Delight yourself in the Lord, and He will give you the desires of your heart.   .
Expand your thinking; all things are possible,
if you only believe.
On the canvas of your mind, paint your dreams, goals, and desires.
It's time for the vision to come to pass;
Witty inventions, designs, concepts, manifest now.
You have an anointing to create.
Write the vision and make it plain, so that people can run with the vision.

Daughters of Destiny and Purpose

It is time; this is the season, woman of God.
Destiny and purpose call you forth.
Thus saith the Lord, come.
Thus saith the Son, come.
Thus saith the Holy Spirit, come.
This is the atmosphere for increase.
The ground has been prepared and is ready.
Greatness is in you; walk into what God has called you to be.
The enemy comes to kill, steal, and destroy, but God came to give you abundant life.
The fruit of the Spirit is actively working on your behalf.
Purpose is mapped out for you.
Destiny drives you toward your purpose.
The Word of God guides you to stay on point.
The Holy Spirit leads you daily as you seek Him.
Walk into what God has designed for you to become.
God is your Creator, Designer, and Coach.
God will lead you and cause you to prosper.
Trust in the Lord, and lean not on your own understanding.
It is time, and this is the season for promotion.
Greatness, destiny, and purpose are propelling you forward.
You are formed, fitted, and fashioned in His image and likeness.
You were called from your mother's womb.
You are an original; there is no one like you.
Fulfill what you were created to be.

Delay Is Not Denied

I waited patiently on the Lord.
God's word is true and forever settled in heaven.
It will come to pass, if I believe and do not doubt in my heart.
God's timing is not my timing.
Whatever was promised, will come to pass.
I must trust, lean, and rely on the Lord.
He is truly my rock and my fortress;
in Him will I trust.
The path that the Lord has chosen for me will open;
It unfolds before me as I seek Him.
The Lord always wants the best for me.
He leads me like a shepherd leads his sheep.
He leads me besides still waters.
He restores my soul.
Surely goodness and mercy follows me all the days of my life.
The table that he prepares before me, my enemy can't stop.
Blessings of the Lord make me rich and add no sorrow.
Delay is not denied.

Don't Mourn for Me

I was born for a purpose, for a reason.
I was only here for a short time.
The enemy came to deceive; but Jesus came for me to believe.
I gave my heart to Jesus on Sunday.
The Word of God pricked my heart.
The seeds were planted and sown into my life.
Even in the midst of trouble, Jesus said He would never leave or forsake me.
So, don't mourn for me.
Others need to know that Jesus is the way to go.
The world is full of different paths to follow.
But Jesus is the way and the truth, today and tomorrow.
Don't mourn for me.
Accept Jesus Christ today, and make him Lord of your life.
Tomorrow is not promised, but you will have everlasting life.
He will wash you clean and come into your heart.
He will be Lord of your life and help you make a brand-new start.
So when you think about me, think about Jesus who set me free.

Dreams

I am a dreamer; my dreams are manifesting now.
I declare and decree a thing, and it shall be established.
I was fearfully and wonderfully made in my mother's womb.
I was called out of darkness into the marvelous light.
I see my dreams and visions coming into fruition.
God molded me and shaped me to succeed.
I have my callings, purpose, plans, and destiny.
My purpose shall be fulfilled.
I see my future; it shall come to pass.
I will not give up, I will not stop, I will not quit.
I will not stop believing; I will press toward the mark of the higher calling in Christ Jesus.
God has designed my future to be bright.
God has called those things that be not as though they are.
God sees me in the future, not my present or my past.
I will achieve, I will believe, I will accomplish all that God has called me to do and to become.
I am a dreamer.

Encourage Yourself in the Lord

The joy of the Lord is your strength.
Weeping may endure for a night, but joy comes in the morning.
No one knows when your morning will come, but you must pursue it
like a deer pants after the water brook, you follow after Christ.
Sing songs of deliverance unto the Lord.
Read the Word of God.
Declare and decree that the battle is over.
Give God praises; see yourself coming out of the situation.
We all go through things in life, don't stay stuck.
Keep moving.
God's promises are true and will not lie.
Hold on until your changes come.
Life and death are in the power of your tongue.
Speak life to your circumstances.
Every day is not sunny; some days are cloudy and rainy, but the sun will shine again.
Let the Son of God rule and reign in your heart.
The power to overcome is in your mouth.
Encourage yourself in the Lord.
You will do and be whatever you say.
See the positive, not the negative.
Encourage yourself until you get to the other side.

Expand Your Wings

This is the season, this is your time.
You have been faithful in the house of the Lord.
You have given much to the kingdom of God.
You were faithful in everything you put your hands to do.
Now it's time to spread your wings and fly.
Soar like an eagle; the territory is yours to possess.
The blessings of the Lord make you rich and add no sorrow.
So, my child, rejoice;
This is your due season.
Do not fear, for fear comes from the enemy.
Take new territory; expand your vision.
I will be with you and will guide you with my right hand.
Favor will follow you as you pursue your purpose and destiny.
You are well able to recover and possess all that was promised.
This is your time to shine.

Abide in the Vine

I must abide in the vine, like a branch abides in the tree.
As long as I abide in Jesus, I will bring forth much fruit.
If I don't abide in him, I will wither away.
My strength is in the vine.
My health is in the vine.
My hope is in the vine.
My life is in the vine.
All that I have need of and desire is in the vine.
I produce fruit because I abide in Jesus.
I'm nourished as I abide in the vine.
I'm sufficiently supplied; all my needs are met.
I'm protected under the shadow of the Almighty.
Just like a tree gets its nourishment from the roots,
I'm provided for as I abide in God's kingdom.
My root system goes down deep in God's word.
I'm like a tree planted by the rivers of loving water.
I shall not be moved; I abide in the vine.

Amazing Grace

Father, your grace is so amazing to me.
I was lost, with no direction.
You never gave up on me.
You watched over me, when I didn't even acknowledge you.
I was living my life with no regrets.
No thought of consequences of my wrongdoing.
You patiently waited for me to come to you.
I was accepted in the family of God.
Grace opened the door for me to walk in.
Love was the key that unlocked the door.
Mercy allowed me to find my way safely.
Forgiveness directed me home.
Father, your grace is amazing to me.

Anointed to Prosper

I am anointed to prosper in every area of my life.
Nothing missing, nothing broken, and nothing lacking.
I am a blessing to others.
The blessing follows me wherever I go.
I am a giver; I love being a blessing.
Increase is in my life; it covers me like an armor covers a soldier.
The anointing surrounds me.
Give, and it shall be given, pressed down, shaken together, and running over.
The anointing to prosper is like electricity;
current flowing from one avenue to another.
It flows and grows as I obey the Lord.
The blessing empowers me to do the work of the kingdom.
Prosperity is not selfish; it's an attitude of gratitude.
Anointed to prosper is doing kingdom business in the world's economy.

Expectant Faith

Faith is the substance of the things hoped for, the evidence of things not seen.
Have an expectancy of receiving your harvest.
You expect your money to multiply in the bank; how much more should your money to multiply
in the kingdom of God.
God delights in the prosperity of his children.
Give, and it shall be given is a law; the law works for givers, not takers.
Just as a farmer plants his seeds and expects a harvest of crop, so should you expect a harvest
when you sow your seeds into the kingdom economy.
If you expect nothing, you will receive nothing.
Have an expectant faith that you will receive.
Give joyfully and not grudgingly; God loves a cheerful giver.
You will always get a return on your investment.
In the kingdom of God, there's no crop failure.
You will always increase on your investment because of good ground.
Exercise your faith muscles, and watch your faith become strong and mighty.
Sow, and you will reap is a law in God's economy.
Believe, and you will receive.

Failure Is Not an Option

Failure is not an option.
I will not quit; I will not stop.
I will recover; I will conquer and complete every assignment.
I will not fail; failure is not an option.
I press toward the higher calling in Jesus Christ.
My eyes are focused, my ears are in tune, my mouth speaks positive things.
My heart is set, my feet walk in the path of righteousness.
My hands are busy working in the kingdom of God.
The race set before me is steady; the Holy Spirit leads me beside still waters.
Failure is not an option; I will pursue and overcome all setbacks.
I exercise my faith to build muscles.
The race is not given to the swift, but to the one who finishes to the end.
I speak to the mountain, and it shall be removed.
I shall have what I say; it will come to pass.
My setback was a setup for a comeback.
I will achieve everything that God has planned for me.
I look unto Jesus, who is the author and finisher of my faith.
Failure is not an option.

Favor

Favor covers you like a shield.
Favor awaits you as you awake.
Favor is on your left and right.
Favor is in the front and rear.
Favor takes you to work each day.
Favor follows you to and from your destination.
Favor follows you all day long.
Favor causes you to excel in every arena.
Favor helps you make right decisions in the marketplace.
Favor protects you and your family from harm and danger.
Favor watches over you as you sleep and slumber at night.
Favor makes you an overcomer.
Favor causes you to operate in excellence.
Favor makes you a winner.

Favor of God

God's favor is upon me.
I didn't qualify for it;
it was granted unto me.
I didn't earn it; it came because of obedience.
The doors of opportunity are open now.
Blessings are surrounding me like a flood,
touching all areas of my life.
God's favor is upon me;
I can't deny it.
My Father lovingly gave it to his child;
it's part of my inheritance.
I'm not trying to be arrogant;
just basking in God's love that flows evenly.
Nothing missing, nothing broken, and nothing lacking.

Finish Your Course

Your Father created you,
Wonderfully and fearfully made.
He knew you before you were formed in your mother's womb;
He blew the breath of life into your lungs.
You are a work of art, crafted by the Master's hand.
Father God has plans for you to succeed and not fail;
You are the apple of his eye.
You have been given all the tools needed to run this race.
The enemy comes to steal, kill, and destroy,
But Jesus came to give you life, and life more abundantly.
Your course is unique, just like your handprint.
The race you run will depend on your faith.
Have godlike faith, and faint not.
Wisdom and knowledge are the important factors.
The gifts of the Spirit will be useful in this race.
Trust in the Lord, and lean not to your own understanding.
You have fought the good fight of faith.
You are victorious.
You have finished your course.
Father God will say, well done, thy good and faithful servant;
Enter into thy rest.

Free

I am free because he whom the Son sets free is free indeed.
No chains can bound me or hold me captive.
I'm free from sickness; I'm whole.
I'm free in my mind, body, and spirit.
I'm not bound; I'm loose.
I'm not down; I'm up.
I'm not a captive to sin; I'm free.
I'm not broke; I'm blessed.
I'm not in turmoil; I have peace of mind.
I am free to walk into my inheritance.
Free to be all that God has called me to become.
Empowered to prosper in every area of life.
I am free to tell everyone the good news gospel.
Yes, I'm free, and free indeed.

Freedom Has a Voice

Freedom is priceless; freedom cries out against injustice.
It can't be bought, but must be sought.
It is sometimes silent and holds its peace.
It moves without being noticed.
Sometimes freedom is bold and vociferous;
it can be heard from far and near.
It has a voice that is clearly stated, never misunderstood.
It is justice for all men and women, every boy and girl.
Freedom is fair; it is for every creed, color, and race.
It is colorblind; all are welcome.
It cries out for those who are bound.
It wants all captives to be set free.
Freedom is powerful; freedom roars like a lion.
It rings from every mountaintop, every valley.
It rings from every courthouse, every church.
It rings from every nation, every culture,
Let freedom ring! Freedom is for the poor and the rich.
It won't be stopped; it won't be pushed aside.
It won't be stopped; it won't be hushed.
It won't be shut down; it won't be quieted.
Let freedom ring! Freedom is priceless.
Let freedom ring from every village, every community.
Let freedom ring from every city, town, and municipality.
Let freedom ring from every state, every jurisdiction.
Let freedom ring! Freedom has a voice; it cries out, let freedom ring!

Fruit of the Spirit: Heaven's Grocery Store

Fruit of the Spirit is like walking down the aisle of a grocery store;
It is up to you to pick the fruit and walk in it.
The first aisle is *love*.
Love is very powerful and is needful in the body of Christ.
All men will know that you belong to Christ because you walk in love.
The next aisle is *joy*.
The joy that you have is given to you by the Lord.
We are to share this joy with others, to bring them into the body of Christ.
The next aisle is *long-suffering*.
We need to be long-suffering with those who do not know Jesus as their Lord.
The next aisle is *gentleness*.
We need to have gentle spirits; not to be doormats,
but to let people know that we represent Christ on earth as he is in heaven.
The sixth aisle is *goodness*.
This is a very important fruit.
We are to let the fruit of goodness show in our walk; we are not perfect,
but we want to let this fruit shine.
The next aisle is *faith*.
Without faith, we can't be effective witnesses.
Faith is the substance of things hoped for and the evidence of the things not seen.
The next aisle is *meekness*.
To be meek is to have a kind spirit and not be mean to people.
The last aisle is *temperance*.

Temperance is having patience with others because Jesus is patient with us.

This store is more special than any other store.

This store is the store of life.

Many times we only have one chance to exhibit our fruit to others.

We need to show our fruit to the lost and draw them into the kingdom.

Make sure your fruit is fresh and effective.

Water it daily with the Word of God, and fertilize it with prayer, praise, and thanksgiving.

As you share your fruit, you will produce more.

Heaven's grocery store is always open.

As we freely receive, we freely give.

God's Timing

There is a time to be born,
A time to die,
A time to sow,
A time to reap,
A time to increase,
A time to decrease,
A time to laugh,
A time to cry,
A time to rejoice,
A time to sorrow,
A time for the sun to shine,
A time for rain,
A time for light,
A time for darkness,
A time for mercy,
A time for judgment,
A time for abundance,
A time for famine,
A time for peace,
A time for war,
Seconds turn into minutes, minutes into hours;
Hours turn into days, days into weeks;
Weeks into months, months into years.

God's Visionary

I am a visionary for the Lord; I speak the Word until it manifests.
God has given me dreams, visions, plans, and promises.
I speak the Word, with faith, purpose, and power.
Faith comes by hearing; hearing, by the Word of God.
Faith is the substance of things hoped for and the evidence of things not seen.
Without faith it is impossible to please God.
I use faith muscles to propel me toward my destiny and purpose.
I seek the Lord for direction; as the Lord leads, I will follow.
Write the vision and make it plain, so that whomsoever reads it can run with it.
The vision isn't complicated; God is not the author of confusion.
The vision is a plan to increase the kingdom of God.
God uses his visionaries to be a blessing to the household of faith.
In these last days, God's people will join forces and become one mind, one mouth, and one purpose.
We will be on point and synchronized as one body for the end-time harvest.
This is not the time to be separated; we are unified, justified, as we work together toward God's vision.
The harvest is plenty, but the laborers are few; go ye, therefore, saith The Lord of Hosts, the fields are ripe and ready for harvest.

He Arose

Jesus died on Calvary's cross.
He died for your sins and mine.
Thirty-nine stripes were laid upon his back.
He was pierced in his hands, his side, and his feet.
A crown of thorns was placed on his head.
For our sins, he died and bled.
They laid him in a borrowed grave.
A stone was placed outside the tomb.
Jesus went to hell, and took the keys of death and hell,
He set the captives free.
On the third day, he rose.
Jesus arose, with all power and authority in his hands.
Jesus paid the price that we couldn't pay.
Jesus was the sinless Lamb.
He arose, He arose, He arose from the dead.

Heroes of Faith

Many have fought and died for America; the land of the free and the home of the brave.
Names of many we don't even know or remember,
But they fought bravely for our freedom.
Blood was shed on this land of the free,
We bless the United States of America with glee.
We have rights and privileges to enjoy,
Even as our military goes around the world employed.
They protect our land and keep us free,
So that we enjoy peace and freedom from sea to shining sea.
Pray for our heroes every day,
Pray that God's hand would be upon the USA.
Freedom is not free; it is a costly commodity.
So let's celebrate our heroes of faith; may God cover them with mercy and grace.
We ask the Lord to cover our men and women in the military around the world,
As we enjoy our rights and privileges; for every man, woman, boy, and girl.
God bless America.

Glory of the Lord

The glory of the Lord is here,
His presence is so very near.
The sweet-smelling savor is present,
The glory cloud is evident.
We worship You in spirit and in truth,
We praise You for all You will do.
You are our everlasting Father,
The King of glory,
The Rock of Ages,
The beginning and the end, oh so holy.
The glory of the Lord is here,
We can feel it in the atmosphere.
He is near as we glorify His name;
With our mouths, we give Him all the praise,
Our hands lifted up and raised,
Our hearts filled with thankfulness and grace.
We come of one accord,
Giving thanks to the King of Kings and the Lord of Lords.

Empowered to Prosper

I am empowered to prosper.
Lack has no control over me.
I abide under the shadow of the Almighty.
I cast down vain imaginations.
My mind is set like concrete.
My heart is full with thanksgiving.
My mouth is full with praise.
My feet are like hind's feet.
I leap and dance in the presence of my Lord.
I make a joyful noise unto the Lord.
His praise will continually be in my mouth.
The Holy Spirit leads me on the path to go.
Where He leads me, I will follow.
His ways are not mine; His thoughts are not mine.
I inquire of Him to lead and direct my paths.
I am empowered to prosper.

Encounter of the God Kind

You are about to encounter the God kind of experience.
The Word of God is powerful, sharper than any two-edged sword!
You have gone through much turmoil,
But this day is the day of deliverance!
Your time has come, saith the Lord!
This is the day that the Lord has made;
You will rejoice and be glad in it.
The trouble has been great, but your deliverance is greater!
You have been through a season of lack.
This day, lack is broken over your life;
You will walk in abundance, starting now!
This is a season of reaping abundance!
The rain is falling; all troubles are gone!
Your joy is returning to you now in
Jesus's name!
Open your mouth, and begin to praise your Lord, your God!
You have the victory! The victory is in your praise!
As you open your mouth, the enemy must flee.
As the praises go up, the blessings come down.
The captive is set free today!
Shackles are broken; chains are falling off.
Let the healing begin.
Deliverance is in this place now, in Jesus's name!
This is the year of the Lord's release!
You are free today; let the redeemed of the Lord say so now!

I Be Free

No ship, no chains, no slave master could bind me.
No plantation, no foreman could hold me.
I be free!
No whippings, no hangings, no amputations.
No bounty hunters, no slave blocks, no threats, no collars.
I be free!
No classification, no name-calling will hinder me.
I be free!
No misrepresentation, no misunderstandings, no racial slurs.
I be free!
No separation, no segregation or integration will stop me.
I be free!
I am wonderfully and fearfully made in the image of God.
I be free!
I was lost; living in sin and bound for hell.
I be free!
I opened my heart and accepted Jesus Christ as Lord and King.
I be free!
Now all men, women, and children have liberty.
Everyone can be free.
He whom the Son set free is free indeed.
I be free!

I Am Woman

I am woman.
I've been a daughter, a sister, an aunt, a wife, a mother, and a grandmother.
I am woman.
I've been a helpmate, an employee, a stay-at-home mom, and a business owner.
I am woman.
I've been single, married, divorced, and widowed.
I am woman.
I've been underrated, overrated, educated, and ignored.
I am woman.
I've had no rights, some rights, and now, equal rights.
I am woman.
I've had bad times, good times, depression, and oppression.
I am woman.
I've been downtrodden, overlooked, admired, and desired.
I am woman.
I am bone of his bone and flesh of his flesh.
I am woman.
I was made from his rib and formed in the image of God.
I am woman.
I've been destined, determined, designed, and developed for greatness.
I am woman.
I have a purpose, a plan, and a place in the kingdom of God.
I am woman.
I am strong, courageous, vibrant, and beautiful.
I am woman.

Harvest Time

The fullness of time has come.
It's time to reap and not faint.
You have sown seeds during the winter, spring, summer, and fall.
A perpetual harvest has come forth.
Get in position for the blessing.
Favor has come upon you now.
Be strong and courageous; fear not.
Gather the spoils, my children.
The blessing of the Lord is upon you.
Rejoice, for harvest time is now.
The fields are ripe for harvest.
This is the season to go forward; do not look back.
You are blessed in the city and the field.
Everything you put your hands to is blessed.
The manifestation is now; do not remember the former things.
This is a new day and a new time.
You are above and not beneath.
You are the head and not the tail.
Dreams, visions, and ideas are bursting forth.
What seemed to be impossible is now possible.
You cannot be denied; this is your season.
This is your inheritance.

Healed, Delivered, and Whole

By Jesus's stripes, I am healed.
I am made complete in Him.
Every area of my body is whole.
Nothing in my life is lacking, broken, or missing.
I walk in the power of God's word.
The work that God started, He will finish.
I stand on the Word of God.
The Word is more powerful than any two-edged sword.
The Word will cut away sickness and disease.
The Word brings me wholeness in body and peace of mind.
I declare and decree that I am healed.
I speak the Word until it manifests in my body.
I walk by faith and not by sight.
Every part of my body must obey the healing of the Word.
The healing power of God is actively working.
Every cell, tissue, and bone will align with the healing power of the Most High God.
God made me fearfully and wonderfully.
I am healed, delivered, and whole in Jesus's name.

It Is Time

This is the appointed time for the body of Christ.
It is our season to shine.
Arise and shine, for the light is come and the glory of the Lord will shine upon you.
I speak life and not death, blessings and not curses.
I think on things above and not beneath.
I walk in the blessings of the Lord.
The Lord is the portion of my inheritance.
He maintains my lot.
My Father shows me the path of life.
In his presence is fullness of joy.
Lack is broken over my life.
Abundance is falling like rain.
Overflow is reigning in my life.
The law of increase is working on my behalf.
Favor is on my right and my left.
Goodness and mercy follow me all the days of my life.
My destiny unfolds before me.
The blessing of the Lord makes me rich and adds no sorrow.
The favor of God surrounds me.
I lack no good thing.
God is great, and greatly to be praised.
His works are wondrous in my sight.

He Touched Me

Jesus touched me and made me whole.
He cleansed me from sin and shame.
I was downtrodden, and he made me whole again.
My body was racked with sickness and pain.
My mind was so distraught, but now I'm sane.
Jesus knew me and called me by name.
He touched me when I was lost in sin.
The devil had me bound, but Jesus freed me again.
I was depressed and oppressed.
Jesus delivered me out of my mess.
He touched me from my head to my feet.
I will tell everyone of Jesus's goodness and grace.
I will spread the good news, from place to place.
Jesus can touch you and change your life.
He can deliver you from all of your strife.
Call upon his name, and he will make you whole again.
Don't run away, but run to him.
Jesus is the only answer for deliverance from sin.
He will wash you clean, whiter than snow.
He will set you on a path for you to go.
Jesus touched me and made me whole.
For him I live and will be so bold.
I will never be ashamed of what Jesus has done for me.
I was bound, but now I have liberty.

It's Not About You

You have been called out of darkness into his marvelous light.

God's hand is upon you.

You have gifts, talents, and abilities especially given to you.

It's in your DNA, graphed inside of you.

You need to use your tools for the kingdom.

The doors of opportunity are open to raise you up.

This is the season for your gifts to be showcased.

Do not underestimate the calling that is upon you.

Not by might, not by power; but by the Spirit of the Lord.

Favor is surrounding you like a shield.

Favor will close doors that need to be closed.

God will place people in your path to uphold you.

Your gifts are needed in the marketplace.

It is time to soar like an eagle; the time is now.

Spread your wings, set your sight high, never look low.

Failure is not an option.

It's not about you; it's about what God has called you to do.

Walk into your destiny.

He who started a good work in you will complete it.

Journey of Life

First, you were a thought in God's mind;
He formed you in the realm of the Spirit.
Then, you were formed in your mother's womb;
Fearfully and wonderfully made.
You were one of a kind, unique in every way;
Your DNA was designed for you only.
Then, you came into this world;
Designed to fulfill destiny.
There is no one like you;
You were born for such a time as this.
You weren't born too early or too late;
It was your time to be born.
You have an assignment to walk out;
Gifts and talents are engraved in you.
You are chosen to be a blessing to others;
You are here to mark time, not just to waste time.
The dash is your birth date and your death date;
Make your dash count.

Justified

I am justified, as if I had never sinned.
God's grace is sufficient for me.
My Lord is my defense attorney.
Jesus went to the cross for your sins and mine.
He took thirty-nine stripes upon his back.
He bled and died on Calvary's cross.
He arose on the third day.
He took the keys of death and hell.
He ascended to the right hand of God, the Father.
He pled my case; now I'm found not guilty.
Jesus has never lost a case.
Now I'm sanctified, justified, and made complete in him.
I'm whole, washed by the blood of the Lamb.
My sins are in the sea of forgetfulness.
I was lost, but now I'm found.
I was bound, but now I'm free.
I was a woman with many life issues.
Now I'm free, with purpose and destiny.
You can be justified too; there is plenty of room for you and me.
Jesus is not a respecter of person.
Everyone is welcome in his court.
You can be justified too.
The blood of Christ has never lost its power.
The blood washes away our sins; nothing but the blood of Jesus.
The blood makes you whole again; wonder-working power
in the blood of the Lamb.
You are justified and made whole again.

Kingdom Movement

There is a movement in the kingdom of God.
We are not satisfied for us four and no more to be blessed.
Increase is in our DNA, we are prosperous without measure.
Prosperity is falling like rain; this is the year of exceptional blessing.
The blessing is for kingdom business; money is needed to bring the lost into the kingdom.
Inventions, witty ideas, and concepts will increase.
We will dominate in the marketplace in all areas.
God has given us wisdom, knowledge, and understanding of the times.
The world is looking for answers.
There is a kingdom sound; there is a movement upon the earth.
It is time for God's people to rule and reign.
The Word of God gives light.
There is treasure in these earthen vessels.
There is intercession of prayer going forth.
There is a shift in the atmosphere.
Favor is covering God's people like a cloud.
As we pray on one accord,
The movement is getting more powerful.
The blessing is coming forth, from the north, south, east, and west.
This is the time for God's children, kings, and priests to take authority in the kingdom on earth as it is in heaven.
I hear the sound of kingdom movement.
We are marching with one mind, one mouth, one purpose.

Lead Me

Lead me, oh Lord, for on my own, I would stray;
Lead me, oh Lord, as I go about my way.
I need you every minute of each day;
Your guidance is needed, lest I will stray.
Holy Spirit, be my compass all day long;
For the devil will cause me to go on my own.
My way is not your way at times.
Give me grace to be in alignment;
I need you to propel me to my assignment.
Many need to be touched by you every day,
As we go about our business along the way.
I won't forget to listen to your voice;
As you lead me on the path to go,
I will rejoice as I follow.

Love Is

Love is kind.
Love is gentle.
Love is patient.
Love is forgiving.
Love does not hurt.
Love does not destroy.
Love does not accuse.
Love does not scar.
Love is calming.
Love is genuine.
Love is sincere.
Love is faultless.
Love does not put down.
Love does not cause confusion.
Love does not hate.
Loves does not enslave.
Love is harmony.
Love is sweet.
Love is joyful.
Love is peace.

Man of Valor

I impact the world for good.
I am called to greatness.
I was birthed into the world to lead.
I bring others into the kingdom of God.
I am a mighty warrior for the Lord.
I am a leader and not a follower.
I achieve everything that I set out to do.
Favor follows me daily.
Goodness and mercy follows me also.
I inquire of the Lord, and He directs my path.
I am a leader in my family, church, and community.
I am a great son, husband, and father to my family.
I provide for my family; there is no laziness in me.
I accomplish my goals and dreams.
I compel many to be saved; none will be lost.
I am a warrior in the kingdom of God.
I have a mandate to win souls for the Lord.
There is a generation of men seeking the Lord.
I war in the Spirit, praying daily.
I battle in intercession for my family.
I declare and decree that I am a man of valor.

Matter of the Heart

This is a matter of the heart,
Not the heart that pumps blood into your body;
This is your spiritual heart,
The inward man;
For where your treasure is, that is where your heart is also.
Your wishes and your desires;
You must keep your heart pure and clean.
The enemy will come to deceive you,
But keep your heart pure with the
integrity of God's word.
The Lord will lift up your countenance,
and give you peace in your heart and life.
Don't hold hate in your heart for anyone;
It will hinder your fellowship with the Lord.
Don't grieve the Holy Spirit;
Release the hurt, pain, and anger.
Our bodies were not designed to carry pain inside.
Release the people, issues, and problems;
Give them to the Lord.
Seek the Lord your God, and you will find him.
Love the Lord with all your heart, mind, and soul;
Your entire being.
Blessed are the pure in heart,
For they shall see God.
You must be kindhearted, sweet spirited,
Self-controlled, peaceful, and worthy of respect;
All these things produce much fruit.

I Samuel 2:1

My heart rejoices and triumphs in the Lord
My strength is lifted up in the Lord
My mouth is opened wide to speak boldly against
My enemies
Because I rejoice in your salvation

Deuteronomy 4:9

Only pay attention and watch yourselves closely
So that you do not forget the things which your eyes
Have seen and they do not depart from your heart
All the days of your life
Make them known to your children and your
Grandchildren, impressing these things on their
Mind and penetrating their heart with these
truth
It's a matter of the heart

Amplified Bible Version

Mission Possible

I am an agent of change.
Circumstances must change when I come around.
I have the expectation that anything is possible.
I confess what I believe until it comes to pass.
Decree a thing, and it shall be established.
All things are possible to those who believe.
The Word of God is true; God is not a man that he would lie.
I must share the good news of the gospel with all who will listen.
I will show the love of God to everyone.
People will be delivered from darkness to light.
I am an agent of change.
Everyone must hear the gospel of good news.
Better is possible to those who believe and receive.
Situations will turn around when I'm present.
The bound will be free; the oppressed, delivered; the sick healed.
I will witness to the lost, at any cost.
I am an agent of change.

Mommy Dearest

Words can not express what you mean to me.
You carried and brought me into this world to
fulfill my destiny.
You nurtured me through the years, not sparing
the rod and spoiling the child.
You led by example of a godly mother,
Serving the Lord with gladness.
The example was set not to be a friend, but a
guiding light.
You let me know wrong from right, even when
I didn't want to hear it.
You always seemed to be right, completely led
by the Spirit.
You had many roles as I grew up.
I will always remember the values that you taught.
Many things I did not comprehend,
But I learned because life taught me again.
I remember Mother's sayings,
Especially when I needed defending.
The words of wisdom were always so rich,
Really enhanced when I had to go and get a switch.
You showed love by example indeed,
The love of God was planted like a seed.
I did not appreciate everything you did,
Until I was grown with my own kids.
Now I know the value of a mother,
The love and respect is like no other.
I will always cherish the memories.
Mommy dearest,
You are the best and the greatest;
You sowed into my life, expecting nothing
in return but love and honor.
You truly earned the name of *mother*.

Mother's Love

How do I define love?
Love is enduring many hours of labor pains to bring
you into this world.
How do I define love?
Sleepless nights when you awoke me every three hours
for breast-feeding.
How do I define love?
Walking the floor with you when you were sick.
How do I define love?
Crying when you had your first day at day care.
A mother's love is so complex.
She will shower you with kisses and hugs,
and punish you when you misbehave.
Mother will fight for you when you are in danger.
She will walk the floor and pray when you don't
come home on time.
She'll knock you out when you get out of line.
Mother will be your supporter when others turn away.
Mother will love you unconditionally when others
are at bay.
She's your nurse, lawyer, intercessor, and teacher
all wrapped in one.
Praying on your behalf to the Father, Holy Spirit,
and the Son.
Motherhood is a job that you never retire from.
Every mother wants to know that hers was
a job well done.
So when you think of love,
think about Mother—
A name so sweet and dear to utter.

Mother, Grandmother, and Servant

Thank you for being a servant of God,
Willing to serve without regard.
I know your reward will be great,
Because of your willingness and faith.
You are a needed part of the body of Christ,
To help and encourage others by being so nice.
We can use many more like you,
Because there are only a few.
Thank you for serving the Lord with a smile,
You serve with elegance and style.
A humble heart and open hands,
Make a strong servant who will stand.
I thank you once,
I thank you twice;
You have such a spirit, so kind and nice.

My Authentic Self

I am authentic, an original by design.
My Creator shaped and formed me before the sands
of time.
I am fearfully and wonderfully made.
So exquisite and unique, my Father knows me from
my head to my feet.
Everything about me, my Creator critiqued.
He designed me with gifts, talents to use,
not to brag or abuse.
I was made to glorify and praise my Father
in everything I do.
I live as a testament to how He brought me through.
My life is an open book for others to read,
to let others know that He can be their Father indeed.
For God so loved the world that He gave
His only begotten Son,
So no one will be lost, but saved one by one.
I am authentic, an original by design.
My Father knew me before I was formed
in my Mother's womb.
I was born at the right time; not too late,
and not too soon.
My Father knows the hairs numbered on my head.
He even knows my thoughts before the words are said.
I am on the path to success,
because my Father always knows what's best.
He leads me on the path that I should go;
I lean on Him for understanding to know.
My Father can be your Father too;
For He has much love for me and you.

Just open your heart and accept His son,
and your journey with your Father has begun.
He will love you unconditionally from the start,
and change the condition of your heart.
His arms are open wide, to accept you at His side.
My Father is waiting for you to come to Him.
He is so full of love and grace.
It is hard to comprehend;
His love is so vast, it has no end.
You can be authentic, an original by design,
because your Father knew you before the sands of time.

Run Toward Your Destiny

Your destiny awaits you.
Don't wait to fulfill your calling; run, don't walk.
Your destiny is unique, made especially and designed for you.
This is your purpose and plan to accomplish.
Many are called, but few are chosen.
Embrace what God has called you to do.
Celebrate being unique; you are one of a kind.
You were tailor-made for what you are called to be.
Embark on new territory; do not fear.
There are new horizons awaiting you.
Stay on track; don't lose your focus.
Don't cease to possess or produce.
The Lord will send people to help you reach your goals.
You are not an island; all parts of the body of Christ are needed.
The Holy Spirit will give you insight and direct your path.
In all getting, get wisdom, for it is the principal thing.
God has not given you the spirit of fear, but love, power, and a sound mind.
The path has been set.
Run toward your destiny.
Destiny means appointed or predetermined place.
Don't delay, deny, or get distracted.
This is your time to soar.
This is your time and your season.
Your destiny awaits you.
Your destiny is calling you by name.

Set Time

This is my set time.
Favor is on my left and my right.
Favor follows me daily.
I rise up with favor and lie down with favor.
This is my time for increase.
Favor propels me to victory.
The set time is now.
Favor is my front and rear guard.
I push toward my appointed time.
God's word enlightens me.
God sends people to help me in my assignment.
I seek the Lord for instructions.
This is my season.
The time is now.
The joy of the Lord is my strength.
I trust in the Most High God.
I rejoice because my victory is here.
I am not before time or after time, but on time.
I am appointed, anointed, and in alignment
for the blessing; nothing can hinder, hurt, or hold up
what God has for me.
This is the time, the place, and the season for favor.

Spirit of the Lord

Where the Spirit of the Lord is, there is freedom.
Where the Spirit of the Lord is, there is peace.
Where the Spirit of the Lord is, there is healing.
Where the Spirit of the Lord is, there is deliverance.
Where the Spirit of the Lord is, there is wholeness.
Where the Spirit of the Lord is, there is victory.
Where the Spirit of the Lord is, there is sound mind.
Where the Spirit of the Lord is, there is joy.
Where the Spirit of the Lord is, there are blessings.
Where the Spirit of the Lord is, there is faith.
Where the Spirit of the Lord is, there is power.
Where the Spirit of the Lord is, there is abundance.
Where the Spirit of the Lord is, there are miracles.
Where the Spirit of the Lord is, there is grace.
Where the Spirit of the Lord is, there is mercy.
Where the Spirit of the Lord is, there is justice.
Where the Spirit of the Lord is, there is truth.
Where the Spirit of the Lord is, there is promotion.
Where the Spirit of the Lord is, there is comfort.
Where the Spirit of the Lord is, there is unity.
Where the Spirit of the Lord is, there is rest.
Where the Spirit of the Lord is, there is forgiveness.
Where the Spirit of the Lord is, there is gentleness.
Where the Spirit of the Lord is, there is favor.
Where the Spirit of the Lord is, there is increase.
Where the Spirit of the Lord is, there is destiny.
Where the Spirit of the Lord is, there is love.
Where the Spirit of the Lord is, there is harmony.
Where the Spirit of the Lord is, there is harvest.
Where the Spirit of the Lord is, there is everything you will ever need.

Stand Your Ground

Storms of life will come.
Speak to the storms and say, peace; be still.
Health problems will arise.
Say, by Jesus's stripes, I am healed.
Family issues will happen.
Raise up a child in the way he or she should go,
And when they are older, they will not depart.
Financial problems will come.
You are blessed in the city and blessed in the field;
Everything you touch is blessed.
You receive a bad report.
God has not given you a spirit of fear,
But power, love, and a sound mind.
You feel like nothing is going right.
I look not at the thing seen, but I look at the unseen.
You look at your shortcomings.
I am fearfully and wonderfully made;
I am not a mistake.
You feel like you are not loved.
I was bought with a price; God loves me.
He knows the number of hairs on my head.
Storms of life will come.
You need to speak the Word of God in every situation.
Don't let the storms handle you;
You handle them.
Let the redeemed of the Lord say so.
You will have whatsoever you speak.
Stand your ground, with the Word of God.
God's word is sharper than any two-edged sword.
Stand your ground.

Stay in Your Lane

Stay on course in your lane.
Don't get distracted; you have much to gain.
You were created and carved to be an
original design.
You are called out of darkness
into His marvelous light.
God, the Father had you in mind.
You were created just in time.
Don't let others distort your view.
Your lane is just for you.
You are fearfully and wonderfully made;
Beautifully crafted in his image.
When the enemy tries to deter you,
Give him the Word of God in hot pursuit.
Situations may come and go,
But the Lord will lead you in the way to follow.
The race is not given to the swift;
It is given to the one who holds on until the end.
When trials and tests try to slow you down,
Say a prayer for angels to surround.
The Father wants you to be all that you can be;
For you are in God's army.
Stay on course in your lane, in Jesus's name.

Stop the Violence

Let's stop the violence in our neighborhoods, right here
and right now.
Let's stop the drive-by shootings.
Let's stop the jails filled with our young men and women.
Let's stop the unjust killings of our black young men.
Let's stop the teenage pregnancies.
Let's stop the drugs sold to our kids.
This is the time and the place to start a new revolution
in Jesus Christ.
A revolution where we care for one another;
Where we look out for our neighbors;
Where we care about our communities;
Where we help one another to keep our communities safe and clean.
Where we help our young people to stay in school.
Where we start businesses in our communities.
Where we start reading programs for our children.
Where we have proper day care for the elderly.
Where we join together as a unit.
Every part of the body is needed.
We are more effective and powerful working
together than apart.
This is the time.
This is the season, because we care.

Strength for the Journey

Sometimes in life
there is sickness in the body.
Just remember, Jesus paid the price on the cross
for all sickness and disease.
Thirty-nine stripes that he bore for us on
Calvary.
At times you may feel that you can't make it anymore;
But remember the Word of God, for healing.
The Word is powerful;
Sharper than any two-edged sword.
The Word delivers and sets the captives free.
The Word is a healing balm of Gilead;
It soothes, comforts, and strengthens you.
Don't ever give up hope;
The Word of God is true.
Faith is the substance of things hoped for;
The evidence of things not seen.
Hold on to the promises of God
until healing manifests.
God will give you strength for the journey.

Success

Success is determination in action;
Putting footwork to what you believe.
It is stretching beyond what you can see or think;
Dreaming what seems to be impossible.
Bringing impossibilities into reality;
It's believing the unthinkable.
Hoping beyond hope;
Reaching for the goal.
It is trusting in the Lord with all your heart;
Leaning not unto your own understanding.
Knowing that with Jesus Christ,
you can do all things;
Because he strengthens you.
Success is breaking barriers that seem
to be unbreakable;
Pressing toward the higher calling.
Success is knowing that you put Jesus
Christ first.
Acknowledge the Lord, and he will
direct your path.
That is success.

Sufficient Grace

God's grace is sufficient for me.
It is wrapped around me like a coat.
I didn't earn it; it can't be bought.
It is freely given unto me.
I don't take it for granted.
It is precious to every child of God.
I need it in the morning when I wake up.
I need it in the afternoon; I need it in the evening and at night.
I need grace in front of me, around me, and behind me.
Grace is unmerited favor given by God.
Grace led me when I was young and will be with me as I get older.
Goodness and mercy follow close behind also.
God's grace is sufficient for me.

Surrender All

I surrender all to my Lord and Savior.
I give him all of my problems and cares.
I cast my disappointments and hurts, like
a fisherman cast his nets.
I must trust in the Lord with all my heart and lean not on my own understanding.
My God looks high, and he looks low.
He knows my rising up and my down setting.
He knew me before I was shaped in my mother's womb.
He knows the number of hairs on my head.
There is nothing that God doesn't know about me.
How mighty is my God; strong and mighty in battle.
When my way pleases the Lord, he makes my enemies to be at peace with me.
A merry heart is like medicine, but a broken spirit
dries up the bones.
I will cast my cares on the Lord, for he cares for me.
Death and life in the power of my tongue, and I will eat the fruit of it.
I must surrender all to the Lord; he is my strong tower.
Those who run to him will be saved.

Survivor

You are a survivor; you are stronger than you think.
Many people look to you for strength and encouragement.
Survival is in your DNA.
At times you feel that you are about to lose your mind;
But the Father gives you peace and a sound mind.
The Lord sends his ministering angels to comfort and keep you.
You are the apple of God's eye.
You are fearfully and wonderfully made.
The Father loves you unconditionally.
You are called to help others survive.
You are called to minister to hurting people.
People need to know that God is their strength.
You don't know how valuable you are to the kingdom of God.
Sometimes you feel that you don't belong, but that is a plot from Satan.
You are part of the body of Christ.
You are needed, just as all parts make up one body of Christ.
Don't look down, but look up, for your redemption draws nigh.
You are called for such a time as this.
You will be like Moses, leading many to the promised land.
Many will be born again because of your example.
You are a survivor for the kingdom of God.

Thankful Heart

God has been so good to me.
He loves me with an everlasting love.
He loved me before I was formed in my mother's womb.
He loved me when I didn't love him back.
I was lost and doing anything and everything I was big enough to do.
But God's love kept me from harm and danger.
I'm so thankful for a loving Father.
God's love is richer and deeper than any other love.
God's love is pure and untainted; my heart is filled with thanksgiving.
His mercy and love endure forever.
If I had a thousand tongues, it wouldn't be enough
to praise my God above.
My heart is filled with thanksgiving.

The Best Is Yet to Come

Eyes have not seen, ears have not heard what God has prepared for his people.
The struggle is over!
Lack is broken over your life.
The abundance of rain is falling now.
The law of increase is upon you.
The season of sowing and reaping is set forth.
The harvest is plenty, but the laborers are few.
Get in the position to reap blessings.
Look up, for your redemption draws nigh.
Rise and shine, for the light has come, and the glory has risen upon you.
The wait is over!
The field is ripe and ready for the harvest.
You have prayed and sought the Lord.
Your prayers have manifested fruit.
Receive everything that has been promised to you.
God is not a man that he should lie.
His promises are true.
What things you desire when you pray; believe, and you will have them.
The blessing of the Lord makes you rich,
And adds no sorrow with it.
You are the lender and not the borrower.
Increase is in your DNA.
You are successful in every arena.
You have insight for this time and season.
You will reap if you faint not.
Be a wise steward of the blessing.
Invest wisely, and see your harvest increase.
The best is yet to come; thus saith the Lord.

The Blessing

The blessing of the Lord makes you rich and adds no sorrow with it.
It surrounds you like a shield; protects like an armor.
It goes before you during the day.
It gives you inside information at the workplace.
It helps you make wise decisions.
The blessing increases your storehouse.
It enables you to be a blessing to others.
It guides you to make wise investments.
It helps you to get the best deals.
It promotes you to higher heights.
The blessing directs your steps.
It establishes your walk.
It increases your wisdom and knowledge.
It is given freely; you can't earn it.
It is God's children inheritance.
The blessing is always in motion.
It fights your battles.
It flows like a river of waters.
It is selfless, not selfish.
It adds and does not subtract.
The blessing can't be bought.
It is priceless; it is favor.
It is valuable; it is wise choices.
It is worthy; it is weighty.
It is costly; it is majestic.
It is powerful; it is holy.
That is the blessing of the Lord.

The Force of Faith

I believe that I receive by faith.
It is the substance of things hoped for and the evidence of things not seen.
Faith is always moving, either toward you or away from you.
Faith is like electricity; it moves toward a power source.
Strong faith increases power; weak faith depreciates power.
The Word of God strengthens your faith muscles.
Let the weak say, I am strong.
Let the poor say, I am rich.
Let the sick say, I am healed.
Let the oppressed say, I am free.
Speak to the mountain with faith, and it shall be removed.
The force of faith empowers you to prosper.
It empowers you to succeed in every arena.
Faith propels you toward your destiny.
Faith saves you; it keeps you and leads you on the right path.
Just as light illuminates darkness,
Faith destroys doubt and fear; the just shall live by faith.

The Gift

The gift can not be brought or sold.
It is precious, priceless.
It was purchased by the blood of Jesus Christ, the sinless Lamb.
It is given to anyone, at any time.
There is no respecter of person, race, nationality, creed, culture, or economic status.
It is freely given to the rich, poor, downtrodden, or up-and-coming.
It is given to the upper class, middle class, and any class.
It's given to educated and uneducated, alike.
It's given to singles, married people, the young, and the old.
It's given to firstborn, middle, and youngest children.
The gift is for everyone and anyone born in this world.
The gift is not selfish but selfless.
How precious are the feet of those who preach the good news.
All men, women, and children must be saved.
The good news gospel that we must be born again.
We can't enter our mother's womb a second time.
This birth is a birth of the Spirit, not the flesh.
We must believe and receive Jesus Christ as Lord and Savior.
It is the greatest gift of all, to have your sins forgiven.
The gift of eternal life; embrace the gift.
The gift is freely given to all to receive.
This gift is not a pretty package under the Christmas tree.
This gift is for all nations to receive.
Jesus Christ gave his life for you and me on Calvary.
What greater love, what a price paid for us to live
with Jesus throughout eternity.

The Struggle Is Over

I've had struggles in my life.
I've been up, down, and almost to the ground.
I've had upswings, downturns, increase, and decrease.
But the struggle is over.
I've had sickness, disappointments, and problems.
But the struggle is over.
Many are the afflictions of the righteous.
But the Lord delivers me out of them all.
I've been talked about and lied to.
But the struggle is over.
I've been depressed, oppressed, and misunderstood.
But I'm delivered.
I've had many battles, but I am victorious.
The enemy tried to stop my assignment.
But the struggle is over.
No weapon formed against me will prosper.
The word out of my mouth is a weapon against the enemy.
The Word of God is sharper than any two-edged sword.
The devil tried to make me flee.
But I found safety in the Rock of Ages.
The enemy sought to destroy my seed.
But the struggle is over.
I declare and decree a thing, and it will be established.
The struggle is over.

Time of Restoration

There have been hurts, wrongdoings, disappointments, and broken promises.
Now is the time of restoration.
God is restoring what the devil meant for evil.
Now is the time for forgiveness.
Letting go of the past hurts.
Forgiveness is a very important factor for restoration.
Restore means to bring back to the original form.
God wants to bring you back to wholeness.
You no longer remember the hurts of the past.
Think of the many blessings in your life.
Let the pain of the past go.
Now is the time to rejoice.
Now is the time to be at peace with yourself.
Rejoice that you are here for such a time as this.
You have a purpose and a destiny to fulfill.
Walk in what God has planned for your life.
Celebrate your accomplishments.
Forget the struggles.
You are fearfully and wonderfully made.
Your Father God has plans to bless you and not hurt you.
Be thankful that God is merciful and just.
The best is yet to come as you seek the Lord with all your heart.
Let the healing begin and be whole again.
Let the joy of the Lord fill your heart.
You are blessed to be a blessing.

Tribute to Mother

Mother is one of the sweetest names,
A mother's love is always the same.
Even when your mother has to correct you,
She shows you love that is so true.
When others want to put you down,
A mother will defend her child, without a frown.
Your mother always wants the best for you;
She intercedes on your behalf,
Sending prayers through.
There is no other, like a sweet mother.
She is a strong woman with wisdom beyond her years,
Teaching her children because she cares.
No one can take a mother's place,
No one can fill that warm embrace.
So cherish your mother, if she is still here today,
For others can only remember her beautiful face.
A mother is like a rare jewel, so precious to behold,
A mother is priceless, more valuable than silver or gold.
Give thanks for a mother so loving and kind,
There is no other like a mother in your lifetime.

True Friendship

A true friend is one you can always depend on;
True friends don't change like the weather or temperature.
A true friend can't be bought;
True friends love you for who you are, not for what you have.
A true friend loves you when you are up and when you are down;
True friends are with you when you soar high and when you are almost to the ground
A true friend is like fine wine;
True friendship improves with time.
True friends don't always agree with what you do;
They will tell you about the real you.
True friends will tell you when you are wrong and when you are right;
A true friend knows you so well, and has great insight.
True friends will be there for you in a time of need;
A true friend isn't always looking to receive.
A true friend's love for you is real and true;
A true friend will never use your love to abuse.
A true friend is like a jewel that's a rare find;
A true friend will put you back in line.
A true friend is there for you when you are happy
and when you are blue;
But there's no other friend like the Lord Jesus Christ to see you through.
He's with you from birth and all the way through your life;
He will never leave or forsake you.
He's a friend that is closer than a brother;
He's a friend like no other.
He will come to your aid at any time, day or night;
He always has you in His sight.
He watches over His sheep and wants you whole again.

Thank God for a friend in this natural life;
A friend is a shadow or pattern of Jesus Christ.
Two can't walk together unless they agree in life;
They must go down the same path and not be in strife.
Be thankful for true friends, but Jesus will be
there to the end.

Turn It Around

This is my season for a turnaround.
I've had many battles, but I overcame.
I've had ups and downs, but I'm still standing.
I've had more months than money.
But everything must turnaround.
I've had setbacks and setups, but I'm still here.
Some days I thought I wouldn't make it.
But I made it through.
Everything in my life must change.
This is my season for a turnaround.
There are hidden treasures in me
waiting to be explored.
The devil thought he had me, but I got away.
I have dreams, visions, and destiny.
It all must manifest now.
Just like a caterpillar goes through a transformation,
So do I go through a metamorphosis.
This is my season for a turnaround.
I was formed in my mother's womb for such a time as this.
I was called out of darkness into his marvelous light.
Generations before me are cheering me forth into my
destiny.
This is my time, this is my turnaround.
I will soar like an eagle, overcoming all obstacles.
I am focused on my assignment.
Nothing will hinder me.
I fight the good fight of faith.
My weapons are not carnal,
But mighty, through God pulling down strongholds.
This is my turnaround.

Unto Us

Unto us a child is born.
Unto us a child is given.
The government will be on his shoulders.
He will be called wonderful, everlasting Father;
Prince of Peace.
He is King of Kings and Lord of Lords.
He is God with us, Emmanuel.
Born in a manger,
No room in the inn.
Born into this world,
And yet, with no sin.
He came to save the lost from sin and shame.
Jesus came to this earth
sinless and with no blame.
He is the Lamb of God;
Born of the Virgin Mary.
We celebrate his birth on Christmas and every day.
He is the greatest gift,
Better than any gift under the tree.
He demonstrated his love for all to see.
As we celebrate Christmas day,
Remember the reason for the season.

Victorious

You are a winner.
You are victorious in every situation or circumstance.
You overcame by the confession of your mouth.
You are a victor, not a victim.
The enemy comes to steal, kill, and destroy.
Jesus came for you to have abundant life.
You are a conqueror; victory is in your mouth.
Defeat is not an option.
You triumph over every obstacle that comes your way.
Every trial, every problem is defeated.
It's only a matter of time before you will be
victorious, if you faint not.
The enemy is a deceiver; do not believe his report.
Believe the report of the Word of God.
Victory surrounds you like a shield.
The enemy is a defeated foe.
No weapon formed against you will prosper.
Everywhere the enemy tries to attack, he is annihilated.
Angels are at bay
ready to fight against the devil and his demons.
Be careful of the words that you speak;
Life and death are in the power of your tongue.
Speak victory, not defeat.

Victorious Fight

I am victorious in this fight.
I am more than a conqueror.
Everything must bow to the name of Jesus.
I win every battle; I am a winner.
Jesus is my commander and chief.
The Holy Spirit gives me inside information.
I am a child of the Most High God.
As the Lord leads me, I will follow.
I listen intently to his instructions.
The enemy comes as a roaring lion,
seeking those to destroy.
Jesus came that I would have life more abundantly.
I am a victor, not a victim.
My weapon of warfare is not carnal, but mighty, through God pulling down strongholds of the enemy.
The chains are broken over my life.
My family and all those in covenant with me.
Let the redeemed of the Lord say so.
I am victorious in this fight.

What Is a Father?

A father is a man who takes responsibility for the upbringing of his children.
A father is there to nurture, train, lead, and protect his seed.
He is a man who works hard to provide for his family.
He takes time to impart values and good morals.
A father guides his children in the way they should go.
A father won't spare the rod when needed.
He tries to be a good example for his children to follow.
He's not perfect, but through his life he has experienced many things.
A father will take a job that he doesn't want in order to provide for his family.
A father will work hard and long hours.
What is a father?
He's a leader.
He's a protector.
He's a guide.
He's a provider.
He's a man worthy to be called *father*.

What Is Love?

What is love?
Love is a look.
Love is a wink.
Love is a touch.
What is love?
Love is a glance.
Love is a hug.
Love is a smile.
What is love?
Love is endurance.
Love is commitment.
Love is sharing.
What is love?
Love is joy.
Love is peace.
Love is long-suffering.
What is love?
Love is true.
Love is faithfulness.
Love is patience.
What is love?
Love is gentleness.
Love is kindness.
Love is meekness.
What is love?
Love is tenderness.
Love is faith.
Love is everlasting.
What is love?

Who Am I?

Who am I?
I am a child of the Most High God.
I was formed, fashioned, and fitted by design.
Who am I?
I was called into time.
Molded in my mother's womb.
Who am I?
I was chosen for this century, to make a mark in this society.
I am wonderfully and fearfully made.
Who am I?
I am a citizen of the kingdom of God.
I'm blood washed and sanctified.
Who am I?
I am created, craved, and called.
I was born for such a time as this.
Who am I?
I am an ambassador for the kingdom.
I represent Christ on earth, as He is in heaven.
Who am I?
I'm made in the image of God, in His likeness.
I speak blessings and not curses.
Who am I?
I am mankind.

Wisdom

Wisdom is the principal thing.
In all your getting, get wisdom;
It allows you to operate in excellence.
Wisdom increases your productivity;
It expands your knowledge in every area of living.
Wisdom is precious—don't abuse it;
It is not showy or prideful.
Wisdom is not used to put others down—it lifts people up;
It is used as a tool in living.
Use it wisely and cherish it;
Don't be foolish and use it for wrongdoing.
God won't bless you if you use wisdom the wrong way;
It will become a curse, instead of a blessing.
Acknowledge the Lord; rely on him daily.
Know that the Lord gives wisdom; it's not of yourself.
Wisdom is not a mind thing, it's a spiritual thing.
It doesn't come with age, because some older people are foolish and some younger people are wise.
Wisdom is being in tune with the Spirit of God.
Being quiet to hear his voice;
Taking time to commune with him.
Wisdom is the principal thing.

You Came

You came to kill, steal, and destroy;
Jesus came to give me abundant life.
You came to bring trials, tests, and trouble;
Jesus came to raise up a standard against you.
You came to bring sadness and pain;
Jesus came to give joy unspeakable and full of glory.
You came to deceive many;
Jesus came to give the truth of the gospel.
You are a defeated foe;
We are more than conquerors in Christ Jesus.
Your plan has been destroyed;
God's people are mighty and full of his spirit.
We will reign forever in God's kingdom.
The pit of hell will be your home and the home of those you deceived.

My Precious

The day you were born brought so much joy to me;
My eyes were filled with tears so that I could hardly see.
Your beautiful eyes and little nose;
When I looked at you, I was all aglow.
My precious little girl;
I have so many dreams for you to be the best that you can be.
I pray that you will grow up with strength and integrity;
Because God wants that for you and me.
A woman full of grace and style;
Sharing God's love with laughter and a smile.
My precious little girl,
You are all that I hoped you would be;
I'll love you throughout eternity.

Name So Sweet

Mother is one of the sweetest names I know.
A mother's love will follow you wherever you go.
You can't run away from a mother's prayer.
She will keep you from the enemy's snare.
Mother will be your very best friend.
She is in your corner, ready to defend.
No matter what you go through in life,
Your mother will be there to help keep you from strife.
Don't take your mother for granted.
She is a precious jewel, just as the Father God planned it.
So if your mother is still with you today,
Give her a big hug and a big kiss.
For many mothers have gone on and are truly missed.
Happy Mother's Day!

No More Tears

No more tears, because your life was a legacy.
You lived your life to the fullest.
You accomplished goals and dreams beyond imagination.
Everyone was touched by your life.
People were inspired and moved by you.
You were a mover and a shaker among people.
You encouraged everyone in your presence.
Young and old were encouraged to do better.
Better was always possible.
You expected nothing but the best.
Losing was not an option.
Quitting was not acceptable.
Pressing toward the higher calling was expected.
No one would be left behind.
Everyone was special in God's sight.
Your life was enriched with people who loved you.
I celebrate your life.

No Scars

No more scars.
Scars show what battles you have been through.
A warrior is proud of his scars;
They show his victorious battles.
But there are also emotional scars that no one can see;
Scars from past hurts and emotional issues.
These scars are more painful than physical scars;
Physical scars can be removed surgically,
But emotional scars need the healing power of God.
You never forget what caused the scars, but the stinging no longer has power over you.
You are delivered and set free by the stripes of Jesus.
You are healed and made whole.
No more scars.

Open Doors

Doors of opportunity are opened to me now.
I was destined to win, and God's favor is upon me.
I was created, called, and coached for greatness.
As I obey the voice of the Lord, I'm walking toward the open door.
I am empowered, in alignment, and set apart to succeed.
As I move toward the open doors, I make the way for others to follow.
I am blessed to be a blessing to my family, my church, and my community.
The door of opportunity is a pathway to success.
Generations after me will be blessed because of open doors.

My Refuge

You are my hiding place and my refuge.
I run to you when I am afraid.
I put my trust in you, my Lord.
Let the weak say, I am strong.
Let the poor say, I am rich.
Let the bound say, I am free.
Let the sick say, I am healed.
Let the oppressed say, I am delivered.
I rest in your arms, and I find comfort and peace.
When my heart is overwhelmed, I run to the Rock of Ages.
You have prepared a table before me in the
Presence of mine enemies.
My cup runneth over; I am fed with the Word of God.
It nourishes me and strengthens me.
You are my buckler and my shield.
You are my strong tower in whom I will trust.
I rest, rely, and lean on you.
Lord, you are the anchor that keeps me on course.

Past, Present, and Future

I thank God for what He has brought me through in the past.
I thank God for what He is doing in my life right now.
I thank God for what He will do in my future.
God is faithful, a very present help in a time of need.
God transcends time; God existed before time began.
He said, light be, and it was.
He spoke, and created night from day.
He spoke, and separated land and sea.
He breathed the breath of life into mankind.
He spoke to the earth when there was no form and all was void.
God is with me today, and He will be with me tomorrow.
He said that He would never leave or forsake me.
God is my past, my present, and my future.
He is the I am God; He is the Rock of Ages.
He is the bright and morning star; He is the King of Kings.
He is the Lord of Lords; He is Alpha and Omega.
He is the beginning and the end.
God holds me in the palm of His hand.
I will not fear the future;
For I know who holds my future.

Peace

The peace of God surpasses all understanding.
It flows to every part of the body.
Peace brings wholeness and healing.
Peace gives me rest as I go about my life.
It makes my journey pleasant and sweet.
Peace causes me to see the beauty of the living.
Peace flows from my head to my feet.
It makes me rest under the shadow of the Almighty.
As I seek peace and pursue it, it prolongs my life.
The peace of God is contagious.
It moves from one person to another.
Peace encourages me and gives me hope.
I arise in the morning with peace.
I enjoy peace during the day.
I am surrounded with peace in the evening
and rest peacefully at night.
I am satisfied as I walk in peace.
Peace prolongs the days of my life.

Prayer of Faith

The fervent, effectual prayer of the righteous avails much;
When we pray, the angels move into action.
There is warfare in the heavenlies;
The angels harken unto the voice of God's children.
We stand in faith, not in fear.
God never sleeps or slumbers; He watches for prayers of faith.
Faith is the substance of things hoped for;
The evidence of things not seen.
The enemy is a defeated foe;
We plea the blood of Jesus against him.
Whose report will you believe?
We must believe the report of the Lord.
We wage war against the enemy and his demons.
We do not fight a physical fight; our fight is spiritual.
Our warfare is not with guns or arrows;
Our warfare is praying the Word of God.
We have on the whole armor.
We come against power and principalities.
We war against demons in regions around the earth.
We pull down strongholds through our prayer.
We do not have the spirit of fear, but power, love, and sound minds.
We will not back up, shut up, let up, or put up with
the devices of the devil.
The enemy comes to kill, steal, and destroy.
God said that He came, that we would have life,
and have it more abundantly.
We are well able to recover and conquer what
the enemy has stolen.

The Word of God coming out of our mouths is sharper
than any two-edged sword.
It is quick and powerful against the enemy and his allies.
Do not fear;
For greater is He that is on you
than he that is in the world.

Price of Freedom

I be free; no chains holding me.
I go to eat wherever I please; no sign on doors you see.
I drive whatever I want; can't hold me back, as long as my payment is met.
I live where I want to live,
as long as the monthly rent or mortgage is paid.
I send my children to the best of schools;
no segregation rules made.
No more colored-only waiting rooms;
I go to my doctor or hospital of choice.
I'm free to make a choice.
I be free; no more back-door entry for me.
I walk in the front door, with style and ease;
Getting served is now a breeze.
I'm free to worship my Lord with liberty;
I'm free to praise God with others of different race.
Free to go from place to place;
Worshipping my Savior, with power and grace.
I was bound, but now I'm free.
I can go to work and earn a paycheck equally.
No, everything is not perfect;
This world has a long way to go.
But I know that freedom isn't free.
Jesus came to all men, because he whom the
Son sets free is free indeed.
I be free; no chains holding me.

Priceless

Salvation is priceless;
It can't be bought.
It's freely given;
It can't be borrowed or earned.
It was purchased with the blood of Jesus Christ
on Calvary's cross.
It is freely given to all who call upon
Jesus Christ's name.
It is available anytime, anyplace, and any season;
There's no special location or hour.
Grace is given to all who seek His face.
All creed, colors, and nationalities are welcome;
There's room at the cross for everyone.
Salvation is available morning, noon, or night;
Three hundred sixty-five days a year.
Come as you are; no special attire is needed.
It's a matter of the heart.
Great is thy faithfulness.
It's new every morning.
Grace and mercy are available to all.
Jesus is the way, the truth, and the light;
No other way to be saved.
Satan came to kill, steal, and destroy;
Jesus came to give us life,
and life more abundantly.
Salvation is priceless.

Rejoice This Day

This is the day that the Lord has made;
We will rejoice and be glad in it.
This is a new day, a new start.
Make the most of this moment in time.
Your attitude will determine your altitude.
Every morning is a fresh start of the day.
Many open doors are waiting for you.
You can make it or break it, with your state of mind.
All things are possible to those who believe.
Make every moment count; use your eyes of faith,
and see the possibilities.
The joy of the Lord will be your strength;
It will propel you to make the most of your day.
Command your morning to be the best day of your life.
Decree a thing, and it will be established.
Speak blessings, not curses, over your day.
Meditate on the goodness of the Lord,
Binding the devil from causing confusion and strife.
Have expectant faith and be excited about this day.
Put on the whole armor of God as you go on your way.
Again I say, rejoice!

Rise Up in Faith

Faith is the substance of things hoped for;
The evidence of things not seen.
Let faith arise in your hearts today.
Faith is putting footwork to things not yet manifested;
Faith is the glue that holds fast to your goals and dreams.
Faith will push you toward your destiny;
It will drive you to your purpose.
It will propel you to greatness.
Walk out in faith, and believe.
As you press your way, the path will open unto you.
Faith is the building block for God's people of purpose.
Walk into what God has called you to do.
Fulfill your blueprint in the earth.
No one can do it like you;
You are an original;
One of a kind.
Rise up in faith.
If you can believe it, you can achieve it.
All things are possible to those who believe.

I Dream

I dream that one day I will be judged by the content of my character instead of my skin color.
I dream that I will have equal opportunity and equal pay.
I dream that housing will be fair for all people.
I dream that my children will get equal opportunity in education.
I dream that I will get quality health care.
I dream that I will be treated fairly in the marketplace.
I dream that our young black men and women will be treated fairly by law enforcement.
I dream that the jails will not be filled with our young people.
I dream that our teenage girls will not be number one among unwed mothers.
These are my dreams, waiting to manifest into reality.

Hiding Place

You are my hiding place;
When I am afraid, I can run to you.
You protect me from all danger and harm;
You give me peace when trouble is all around.
The peace of God surpasses all understanding;
No weapon formed against me will prosper.
All lying tongues God will condemn.
I run to you, and my life is saved.
You comfort me with loving-kindness.
I rest in your bosom.
The joy of the Lord is my strength.
You prepare a table before my enemies.
You anoint my head with oil, and my cup runs over.
Goodness and mercy follow me all the days of my life.
You cover me with your wings; I abide under the shadow of the Almighty.
You are my hiding place;
I run to you, and I am saved.

Power of Praise

The power of praise is in my mouth.
Bless the Lord, oh my soul, and all that
is within me.
I bless His holy name.
Blessings, not curses, are in my mouth.
I choose blessings.
The Spirit of the Lord is upon me.
I give praise to the Lord with my whole heart.
Come magnify the Lord with me.
Let us exalt His name together
God is worthy to be praised.
I will praise Him in the morning.
I will praise Him at noonday.
I will praise Him in the evening.
I will praise Him at night.
Praise is a weapon against the enemy.
When the praises go up, the blessings come down;
That is the power of praise.

My Healer

Jesus heals me from all of my sickness and diseases.
His grace is sufficient for me.
No sickness shall come upon my body or my household.
I am healed, delivered, and whole.
Nothing missing, nothing lacking, and nothing broken.
I walk in prosperity, body, mind, soul, and spirit.
The peace of God surpasses all understanding.
I set my mind to agree with the Word of God.
The redeemed of the Lord shall say so.
Sickness has no place in my body.
The blessing of the Lord makes me rich
and adds no sorrow with it.
Divine healing is upon me now.
I am healed from the top of my head
to the soles of my feet.
Every part of my body is whole and complete.
Every part is fitly joined together.
The joy of the Lord is my strength.

Women of Grace

Grace surrounds you like a shield;
It has brought you through many trials and tests.
Grace gave you comfort during the hard times;
It kept you form losing your mind.
Your ministering angels watched over when you thought you couldn't make it;
Grace gave you peace of mind when you didn't know where to turn.
Goodness and mercy follow you;
Many doors of opportunity have opened to you because of grace.
You are women of beauty and style; yet you are servants of God to many.
You make others feel welcome and at peace.
Your smiles light up a room.
Your later days will be greater than your former.
Grace looks good on you.

My Child

Don't worry and don't fret;
The best is yet to come.
I'm not a man that I would lie;
I have never failed you yet.
Whatever I have promised will come to pass;
Those things that you desire will manifest.
I am God, and my word is true;
My word is full of promises for you.
Begin to praise and glorify my name,
From the rising of the sun, till the setting of the same;
My name shall be praised.
My promises are true and forever settled in heaven.
I will perform all that I said I would do,
To let the love of God shine through.
Many will see that I am God, and God alone;
I sit in the heavenly upon my throne.
You will be a testimony for all to see
that they will see my glory shining in thee.
Hold on to my promises, and don't let go;
For what you reap will be what you sow.

Make a Comeback

I was lost, but now I'm found.
I was down, but now I'm up.
I was sick, but now I'm healed.
I was broken, but now I'm blessed.
I was last, but now I'm first.
I was bound, but now I'm free.
I was fearful, but now I'm full of faith.
I was depressed, but now I'm happy.
I was oppressed, but now I have peace.
I was set back, but now I'm set up.
I was sad, but now I have joy.
I was silly, but now I have wisdom.
I had a setback, but now I have a comeback.
My comeback is a setup for a blessing.
My comeback is a setup for promotion.
My comeback is a setup for increase.

Masterpiece

My Creator designed me to be a masterpiece.
He knew me before I was formed in my mother's womb.
He knew all about me before I was created; He blew the breath of life into me.
He saw my inward parts.
He called me by my name.
I was born for such a time as this.
This is the season for my destiny.
I wasn't too early or too late.
My Creator has a purpose and a plan for me.
His thoughts are higher than mine.
His ways are greater than mine.
He molds me with artful and loving hands.
I am uniquely made.
There's no one like me; I'm an original.
My DNA is one of a kind.
I'm a masterpiece under construction.
God is molding me and designing me on the potter's wheel.
I am fearfully and wonderfully made.

In the Valley

When I'm in the valley of the shadow of death, I will fear no evil.
God is with me when I go through the valley of issues.
In the valley, I find refuge; He restores my soul.
It's in the valley when I seek His face.
In the valley, I call upon the name of the Lord.
In the valley, I pray earnestly for deliverance.
When I'm in the valley, I press into His presence.
In the valley, the potter shapes and perfects me.
In the valley, I'm formed in His likeness.
In the valley, I decrease so that He will increase.
When I'm in the valley, God collects my tears.
God will never leave or forsake me.
In the valley, I'm comforted by the Word of God.
In the valley, I rest in His bosom.
In the valley, I find joy unspeakable, full of glory.
God prepares a table before me in the presence of my enemies; my cup runneth over.
Goodness and mercy follow me all the days of my life.
In the valley, I am transformed.
In the valley, I'm strengthened and nourished.
In the valley, I come out stronger and wiser.

Image

What you see is what you will be.
Image is a tool to use for where you want to go.
Begin to see greatness in you.
Success is in your DNA.
Failure is not an option.
Write down your goals and dreams.
Inquire of the Lord to direct your path.
You will meet the right people at the right time.
The Lord will direct your path daily.
Always remember the Lord, your God.
He gives power to get wealth.
You have gifts and talents that are needed
in the kingdom of God.
He will give you inventions, ideas, and concepts.
Destiny and purpose are cheering you on.
Character and integrity will keep you on track.
Image is what you see on the inside
before it manifests on the outside.
It's not who you were in the past; it's who you will become
in the future.
You are a work in progress; God is not finished
with you yet.
You are a work of art on a canvas.
God knows your ending before your beginning;
He knows what you will become throughout eternity.

I Exalt Thee

I exalt you, oh Lord, my God;
You are above, not beneath.
I worship and adore you;
I magnify your name.
You are greatly to be praised;
You are beautiful to me.
I behold your goodness and mercy;
You lead me into the green pastures
and beside the still waters.
You restore my soul.
You are my peace;
Your peace surpasses all understanding.
You are my joy.
I bask in your glory;
I rest in your bosom.
You are my righteousness;
Your love is amazing to me.
You are my high priest;
You are my shepherd;
You are my guide.
You love me with an everlasting love.
You knew me before I was formed in my
mother's womb.
You know when I rise up and when I settle down.
You breathed the breath of life into me.
You molded me, like a potter;
I am fearfully and wonderfully made
in your image and your likeness.

Message with a Mission

I am on assignment for the kingdom of God.
I go into the highways and hedges,
Compelling those to come into the kingdom.
Everyone will hear the good news of the gospel;
Many are healed and delivered by the Word of God.
Shackles are broken, and the bound are set free;
Those who are oppressed will be delivered.
The blind will see, and the lame will walk;
The deaf will hear, the mute will speak.
The downtrodden will be lifted up;
Poverty will be destroyed.
Creative miracles shall manifest;
Nothing missing, nothing broken, and nothing lacking.
The good news is freely given;
The Father wants all to be saved,
and none to be lost.
I'm available, on call, on duty, and ready
at all times.
He whom the Son sets free is free indeed.
There is nothing that the blood of Jesus can't conquer.

I Cry

Every man, woman, boy, and girl cry out for help
where there is no joy.
I cry in the dark and quiet room,
Wondering when this storm will end.
I know God didn't cause this to happen to me;
It was the work of Satan, the enemy.
Lord, open my eyes, that I might see
that you only want joy, peace, and liberty for me.
The devil came to kill, steal, and destroy;
But Jesus came to give me unspeakable joy.
I know that you will deliver me and set me free
from every trap that the devil set for me.
Freedom from oppression and depression;
Freedom from low self-esteem.
I cry aloud to my Savior and Redeemer;
He comforts me and guides me along the way.
He dries my tears and strengthens me.
My cry was from pain, but now it is from victory;
He whom the Son sets free, is free indeed.

I Am Whole

Jesus touched me and made me whole.
He cleansed me from sin and shame.
I was downtrodden, and He made me whole again.
My body was racked with sickness and pain.
He touched me, and now I am healed to praise His name.
My mind was so distraught, but now I'm sane.
Jesus knew me and called me by my name.
He touched me when I was lost in sin.
The devil had me bound, but Jesus freed me again.
I was depressed and oppressed.
Jesus delivered me out of my mess.
He touched me from my head to my feet.
I will tell everyone of Jesus's goodness and grace.
I will spread the good news, from place to place.
Jesus can touch you and change your life.
He can deliver you from all your strife.
Call upon His name, and He will make you whole again.
Don't run away, but run to Him.
Jesus is the only answer for deliverance from sin.
He will wash you clean, whiter than snow.
He will set you on a path for you to go.
Jesus touched me and made me whole.
For Him I live and will be bold.
I will never be ashamed of what Jesus has done for me.
I was bound, but now I have liberty.
He touched me.
I was destined for hell, but He set me free.

Power of Worship and Praise

Praise for the Lord is in my mouth.
Worship and praise defeat my enemies.
Praise sends ambush into the enemy's camp.
Praise delivers me out of trouble.
I sing praises to the Most High God.
I worship the King of Kings and the Lord of Lords.
Praise and worship precede the battle.
The battle is not mine; it is the Lords.
The victory is in my mouth.
Praise and worship are mighty weapons.
I am more than a conqueror in Christ Jesus.
The weapon of my warfare is mighty,
pulling down every stronghold of the devil.
I praise the Lord in advance.
I worship before the walls come tumbling down.
Praise and worship cause me to walk by faith and not by sight.
There is power in my mouth.
I shout to the Lord my God.
There is power in my mouth now.
God will deliver His people out of darkness.
We will be transformed into His marvelous light.
As the praises go up, the blessings come down.
I triumph over the enemy, with praise and worship in my mouth.

Rise Up

Rise up, my people,
Come out of the waste places.
It is time to flourish in the land that I promised to you.
It is time to walk into your destiny.
It is time to reap and not faint.
Arise and shine, for your light has come.
The glory of the Lord is risen upon you.
Awake out of your sleep.
Shake yourselves; it is manifestation time.
Take off your mourning clothes; it is time to rejoice.
Your reaping season is now.
You have sown seeds.
You have watered, and now it is time to harvest.
Harvest time is now.
This is the season to reap everything that was promised to you.
The enemy can no longer hinder you.
He is a defeated foe.
You have the victory.
You shall prosper in all areas;
In business, in education, in government, sports, and the arts—
Every arena is now open unto you.
Souls will be saved, the sick healed, the bound set free;
The blind shall see, the deaf shall hear, the mute
shall speak, and the lame shall walk.
The curse of lack is broken.
Oppression is destroyed.
Depression is annihilated
You are appointed, anointed, approved, and in alignment
for the blessing.
Nothing can hinder, distract, delay, or deny you.

It is time to possess the land which I have given to you.
The enemy has tried to distract you,
But he is bound in Jesus's name.
You are empowered to recover all;
Nothing will be left behind.
The famine is over;
The abundance of blessing of the Lord is here now.
You have eyes to see.
Ears to hear.
Mouths to speak.
Hands to reap.
Feet to tread upon.
This is the season to prosper,
Right here and right now.
I declare it and decree it in Jesus's name.

Relentless Praise

I will not stop; I will not give in; I will not quit.
I will bless the Lord at all times.
Praise for him will continuously be in my mouth.
I will praise the Lord morning, noon, and night.
My God is worthy to be praised.
He is the God of the breakthrough.
Things are breaking in the realm of the Spirit.
The kingdom of darkness is under attack.
We war in the heavenlies.
The angels harken to the prayers of the righteous.
We do not war against flesh and blood.
We fight a spiritual war.
Our warfare is not a natural fight.
This fight is a supernatural fight.
We will win; we are victorious.
We are more than conquerors.
The weapons of our warfare are mighty in God.
We pull down every stronghold of the enemy.
We cast down every vain thing that exalts itself against the Most High God.
I will praise the Lord with my whole heart.

Season of Increase

This is the season of increase.
It is the time to reap the harvest.
You have planted and tended; now it is time to pluck up that which was planted.
The crop is ready for harvesting.
Seeds were planted for health, wealth,
direction, wisdom, and dreams.
You have weeded out doubt, unbelief, lack, and naysayers.
Now it is time for increase; the harvest is plenty
but the laborers are few.
You have spoken to the mountain and cast it into the sea.
As the Lord blesses you with increase,
You must sow into the kingdom.
As you bless the kingdom of God,
Your harvest will multiply.
Give, and it will be given to you.
Press down, shaken together, and running over;
Blessed to be a blessing.
As there are seasons in the natural,
So are there seasons in the realm of the Spirit.
You sow different ways in each season.
Be a wise farmer—
Speak over your seeds;
Call in the harvest of increase;
Don't let weeds of worry and impatience into your harvest.
Put the Word of God on your harvesting; just as a farmer would tend to his garden,
so are you to tend to your harvest.
Speak positive words over your increase.

Don't be selfish.
Help your brothers and sisters in Christ;
Show others how to increase their harvest.
There is a cycle of harvesting—
You cultivate the ground;
You then plant your seeds.
Give water, and decree the Word of God over your harvest.
This is the season for increase.

Season of Favor

The season of favor is upon you now.
Favor surrounds you like a shield covers a soldier.
Favor is in front of you and behind you.
Favor is on the right and on the left.
Favor is causing the body of Christ to become
a mighty nation in these last days.
God will increase favor in our lives.
God will make our names great.
Favor will cause the lost to hear what thus
says the Lord in this season.
Favor will bring the lost to hear the gospel
of the good news.
They will be drawn by mercy and loving-kindness.
Favor will cause us to walk in excellence in every area.
Favor watches over us at night and rises up early
in the morning.
Because of favor, we are not selfish.
Because of favor we are selfless.
Favor causes us to be caring for others.
Favor makes us loving and compassionate.
This is the season of favor.

Season of Life

As there are seasons on the earth,
So are there seasons in life.
Winter represents a time when things are dormant;
Things are still, not much movement.
There are dead areas in our lives that need to be cut away—
areas that are not fruitful or productive.
Then comes springtime.
Flowers are budding;
Everything seems to come to life again.
You feel rejuvenated.
You have hopes and desires to start fresh.
You have new plans and ideas for your life;
Desires to improve your lifestyle and become fit.
Then comes summer.
It is time to have fun in the sun.
The weather is beautiful.
Everything is blooming.
You become inspired to do new things.
You are adventurous in travel.
You experience new places.
Fall begins to set in.
The trees start to change colors.
A beautiful array of colors, with rich tones of orange and red.
You begin to relax more and enjoy the changes.
You slow down a little and notice how far you have
come this year.
Looking back over your accomplishments, and looking
forward to things to come.
So as seasons come and go,
Realize that everything must change in life also.

Be mindful that nothing stays the same.
Allow changes in your life to mold you and make you stronger.
Let change make you a better and more productive person.
Use each season to make you enlarge your territory.
Always abounding, be like a stream;
Always moving and increasing.
Never become stagnant,
For seasons come to make you realize that change is good.
Ever increasing favor to use as a tool
to empower you to the next level.
Do not be afraid of change—
Embrace change, and enjoy the journey.

Season of Prayer

This is the season of prayer.
The enemy is rising up against God's people.
We cannot remain silent any longer.
We must cry aloud.
We must call upon the name of the Lord.
We send up prayers into the realm of the Spirit.
The enemy will not defeat the kingdom of God.
No longer will we put up with senseless
killings in America.
We must join forces, together in prayer.
The weapon of our warfare is not carnal.
Our prayers are mighty in God.
The devil is a defeated foe.
We bind him in the name of Jesus Christ.
We pray for the families that have lost loved ones.
We pray that the Lord will comfort their hearts.
We must stand together, arm in arm.
We are stronger together than apart.
We can no longer ignore the crisis in our nation.
Every knee must bow, and every tongue confess that
Jesus Christ is Lord.
There is no other name to call upon.
We must take a stand together now.
All lives matter in Jesus's name.
The killings must stop.
We will no longer tolerate these senseless events.
Enough is enough.
Father, your children cry out to you now.
We need you, Abba Father.
Amen.

The God of More Than Enough

My God shall supply all my needs,
According to his riches in glory by Christ Jesus.
I have more than enough.
I have no lack.
I walk in the flow of increase.
My God loads me up daily with benefits.
I have abundant life.
The Lord is doing marvelous things in my life.
No weapon formed against me shall prosper.
In God's presence is fullness of joy.
The table is set before me in the presence of mine enemies.
God anoints my head with oil; my cups runs to overflowing.
I exalt the Most High God.
I rest in him.
He restores my soul.
The Lord is my and strength and my salvation.
The Lord is on my side; whom shall I fear?
I give the sacrifice of praise and thanksgiving.
I trust in the Lord, not confidence in man.
I shall live and declare the works of God.
This is a season of increase.
This is the year of the Lord's release.

Blessings of Increase

The seven years of poverty is over.
The year of famine is gone.
There will be seven years of plenty.
The land will produce and flourish like never before.
You will receive double for all of your trouble.
Your investments will increase.
This is the time to invest wisely.
Increase is in your DNA.
It flows to all areas of your life.
Be wise like the virgins who had oil in their lamps.
Don't be foolish and spend unwisely.
This is the time to plant into the kingdom.
You will reap a bountiful harvest.
God's word is true and does not lie.

Set the Captives Free

You were bound and headed for hell.
Satan had you confused with lies.
He desired to sift you like wheat.
But Jesus came to set the captive free.
Jesus shed his precious blood on Calvary.
His hands and feet was pierced.
His head had a crown of thorns.
His body was unrecognizable from whippings.
He said not a mumbling word.
Jesus suffered dearly for you and me.
He took the keys of death and the grave.
He died so that we could be free.
He died so that we could serve Him with power and liberty.
What a costly price to pay.
He hung His head and said, it is finished.
Now we are free, and free indeed.
His majesty sits on high, on the throne.
The Father says, come.
The Son says, come.
The Holy Spirit says, come.
Three in one.
The angels are amazed.
What is man that your mind is so full of them?
You were captive to sin.
Now you are free women and men.
You are whole again.

Stand Firm

The winds are raging, and the waters are rising.
It seems like the storms of life are about to overtake me.
I call upon the name of the Most High God.
He is my refuge, a strong tower.
The enemy seems to encamp around me.
I begin to praise my Father and make a joyful noise.
I begin to pray the Word of God over my circumstances.
The situation seems to get worse.
I'm not moved by what I see.
I call those things that be not as though they are.
I confess that I am more than a conqueror.
I declare that I'm above and not beneath.
My feet are firmly planted on the Rock of Ages.
I will stand until my change come to pass.
I rejoice in the God of my salvation.
God is my salvation and my deliverer.
I find safety for God is my portion.
I shall be planted like a tree by the living waters.
I shall not be moved; I shall stand firm.

Greatness

Greatness is not given to the foolish, but to the wise.
It is given to be used properly.
Wisdom is the principal thing.
Greatness is acquired, not required.
Abraham was great, but he lied and said his wife was his sister.
Moses was great, but he stuttered.
Noah was great, but he got drunk.
Joseph was great, but he was hated by his brothers.
Rahab was great, but she was a harlot.
David was great, but he took another man's wife.
The woman at the well was great, but she had many husbands.
Many men and woman in the Bible were great.
Greatness does not mean perfection.
No one is perfect.
Only God—the Father, Son, and Holy Spirit—is perfect.
We all have potential for greatness.
We must develop the tools given to us.
Everyone has a history.
No one's past is perfect.
But one day, we will met Jesus Christ and make him Lord.
Inquire of the Lord, and He will direct your path.
Jesus saves, from the gutter-most to the uttermost.
We all have potential to do great things in the kingdom.
Remember to put God first in every endeavor.
Give God all the praise, for it is He who gives you wealth and adds no sorrow with it.
Greatness is in you.

God of Many Chances

Our God gives many chances.
He knows how frail we humans can be.
He knew you throughout eternity.
Our Father knows you from beginning to the end.
His love for you will never end.
You have made many mistakes.
But his love for you is full of grace.
All of your faults are thrown into the sea.
All God sees is the blood of Jesus covering thee.
His grace is sufficient for all.
Jesus Christ came for you to believe.
He came so that all would have liberty.
God's mercy is for everyone to receive.
There's no one who can't receive God's forgiveness.
Jesus gave his life for all mankind.
His mission was heavenly designed.
God's desire is that all will come to him.
He wants no one to die in sin.
Open your heart and invite Jesus to come in.
You will never be alone again.
God loves you with such love.
His grace and mercy come from above.

God Is Able

God is able to deliver me in the time of trouble.
I cry out to the Lord, and He hears my cry.
He's a strong tower; I run to him, and I am safe.
God is a deliverer.
He's a way maker.
He's my all and all.
He's Alpha and Omega.
He's the first and the last.
He's the beginning and the end.
He's the bright and morning star.
He's our protector.
He's the lily in the valley.
He's Almighty God.
The everlasting Father.
God never sleeps or slumbers.
God is able to do everything that He said he would do.
Every word that comes from His mouth
is true and forever settled in heaven.

God Is

God is Alpha and Omega.
God is King of Kings and Lord of Lords.
God is the beginning and the end.
God is the everlasting Father.
God is the Prince of Peace.
God is the living water.
God is the wheel in the middle of the wheel.
God is the potter.
God is Genesis to Revelation.
God is my all in all.
God is the lily of the valley.
God is a way maker.
God is a strong tower.
God is the bright and morning star.
God is a healer.
God is my help in times of trouble.
God is the salt of the earth.
God is my rock, shield, and salvation.
God is my provider.
God is my fortress.

Fruitful Harvest

I am like a tree planted by the rivers of living water.
I bring forth fruit in its season.
The Word is a fertilizer to my soul.
It feeds me daily so I can remain strong.
I delight in the law of the Lord.
Storms and tests come to deter me from my mission.
I stand firm because my roots are down deep.
I produce in my season.
I will not fail.
I flourish because the law of abundance is working.
I am firmly planted.
I shall not be moved.
My harvest is passed down from generation to generation.
My seed is blessed because I am blessed.
I will not have crop failure.
The harvest is bountifully blessed.
The blessing of the Lord makes me rich and
adds no sorrow with it.

Walk Out Your Dreams

Dreams, desires, and goals will manifest.
Seeds of faith have been planted and watered.
It is time for the seeds to flourish and bring forth fruit.
You have prayed, planned, and prepared.
Now the time has come to harvest.
Step out on the promises of God.
The favor of God is upon you.
It is harvest time.
God has given you inspired ideas, divine connections, great expectations, and open doors of opportunity.
Desire prepared the way.
Determination knocked on doors.
Destiny has cleared the path.
Decree it, and it shall come to pass.
It shall be established in Jesus's name.
Walk out your dreams.

Willing Vessel

God helped me to be a willing vessel.
The joy of the Lord is my strength and adds
no sorrow with it.
Our God is rich in mercy.
I decree a thing, and it shall be established.
I press toward the mark of the higher
calling in Jesus Christ, the Anointed One.
I will walk in my purpose and destiny.
My will is to do the work of my heavenly Father.
Many are called, but few are chosen.
I compel men and woman to come into the kingdom of God.
I call them out of darkness into the marvelous light.
My prayers travel far and near.
I war in the Spirit.
I am a light set upon a hill.
Many will be drawn into the light.
Jesus is the answer.
Call upon his name while he is near.
Jesus is the way, the truth, and the light.
No one comes to the Father except through the Son.
There's room at the cross for me and for you too.

Faithful God

Great is my faithfulness toward you.
I will not leave or forsake you.
I am with you in every situation.
I am with you when you go through hard times.
I hoped that you would listen to my voice,
But sometimes you chose your own way.
I am a forgiving Father.
There's room at the cross for you.
I will turn no one away.
My arms are open wide.
My heart aches when my children don't obey.
My word is for everyone.
It is never too late.
You can always turn your life around.
As long as you have breath and life,
Anything is possible.
My love for you is deeper than the sea.
My grace is sufficient for you.
My mercy is extended toward you this day.
You can always trust me.
I will never turn away from you.
You are my beloved, saith the Lord of Hosts.

Expanding Wings to Fly

I have given you gifts, talents to use in the kingdom.
My calling is without repentance.
That which I have placed in you is unique.
Thus saith the Lord,
You are like a rare jewel, full of many facets.
So beautiful, with many array of colors and design.
You are very special; there is no one like you.
I am the potter, and you are the clay.
I am molding and making you to soar into your destiny.
Look up, for your redemption draws nigh.
Spread your wings and take territory.
I have given you dominion over the earth.
You are called, chosen, and created to lead others.
Become a visionary for this time and this season.
Do not fear, but be full of courage.
Open your spiritual eyes to see the territory that I have given to you.
Expand your wings to fly.

Excellence

I operate in the spirit of excellence.
It shows in my job, business, and school.
I press toward the mark of the higher calling through Jesus Christ.
I inquire of the Lord for direction.
The Holy Spirit leads and guide me daily.
I am empowered to excel in every area.
Wisdom and knowledge enlighten me.
Greatness is in my DNA.
The Word of God gives me light toward my goals.
Purpose and destiny are flowing in my veins.
I won't give up or give in.
I will pursue the plans mapped out for me.
I am positioned for increase.
Favor, goodness, and mercy follow me.
I have dreams, visions, and desires.
I was formed and created for such a time as this.
The plans God has for me are great.
I praise the Lord with my whole heart.
From the rising of the sun to the going down of the same,
I will bless his holy name.
I am fearfully and wonderfully made in his image and likeness;
I am a masterpiece for the kingdom of God.
The Spirit of the Lord is upon me to fulfill his purpose and plans.

Write the Vision

Write the vision and make it plain.
Make it plain so that whosoever reads it can run with it.
Write down the plan for you to reach your destination.
Your purpose and destiny are waiting for you to walk them out.
The Word of God is your GPS; it will guide you on your journey.
The Holy Spirit will keep you on track.
Trust in the Lord with all your heart; lean not on your own understanding.
Write down your goals and dreams.
God has called you to be a producer, not a spectator.
A producer makes things happen; a spectator watches things happen.
You are the only one who can write your own history.
You have been given abilities, goals, dreams, desires, and gifts.
Pursue your vision like a deer pants after the water brook.
Don't grow weary; stay on course.
Don't get distracted.
You will have victories and defeats.
Victory will propel you.
Defeats teach you lessons.
Dare to be a visionary.
The path is prepared;
Walk it out.

Tribute to a Friend

Don't weep for me, because my new life is in glory.
I've been through so much upon this earth,
Suffering with troubles and sickness.
I loved my family and did the best I could.
I loved my church family and served as I should.
Many times my body was racked with pain,
But I served my church just the same.
Don't weep for me, because now I'm whole,
Walking on the streets of gold.
My mansion was made just for me,
Because Jesus paid the price on Calvary.
I'm thankful of everything my family did for me.
May the Lord bless you; you filled my heart with glee;
Don't weep for me, because now I'm free.
No more sickness, no more pain; now I'm giving praises
to God and blessing his holy name.

The Woman at the Well

The woman came to draw water that day;
She came around at noon, to keep others at bay.
Jesus was waiting to meet her at noon;
He knew that she would be there soon.
It was a custom for Jews not to deal with Samaritans,
this was her time and season for an encounter with Jesus.
Jesus told her about the living water;
That she would never thirst again,
That all power and might was in his hand.
What kind of water could this be,
to set any man or woman free?
With natural water, you will thirst again,
But the living water can't be contained.
Jesus told the woman all that she had done;
The woman was with many men, but not married to none.
She repented that day and received the Son;
This living water overflowed her soul.
She ran into town and spread the good news to all—
Come see this man who told me all that I have done;
He must be the Anointed One.
So if you are thirsty and dry,
Give Jesus Christ the Lord a try.
He will fill your empty vessel today;
For He is the truth, the light, and the way.
He will wash you clean and make you whole;
Just like the Samaritan woman,
You will be so bold.

Encounter of the God Kind

You are about to encounter an experience of the God kind.
The Word of God is powerful;
Sharper than any two-edged sword.
You have endured much turmoil,
But this day is the day of deliverance.
Your time has come, saith the Lord of Hosts.
This is the day that the Lord has made;
You will rejoice and be glad in it.
The trouble has been great,
But your deliverance is greater.
You have been through a season of lack;
The devil and his demons were on the attack.
Lack is broken over your life today;
You will walk in abundance, I say.
You will walk in abundance, starting now;
The Holy Spirit will show you how.
This is a season of reaping abundance.
The rain is falling; all troubles are gone.
Your joy is returning to you now.
Open your mouth and begin to praise your Lord.
You have the victory;
As you open your mouth, the enemy will flee.
As the praises go up,
The blessing comes down.
The captive is set free today;
Let the Lord have his way.
This is the year of the Lord's release.
You are free today;
Let the redeemed say so.

You Reign

You reign as Lord and King over this land,
With all power and majesty in your hand.
You are just and true in all your ways;
You are the ancient of days.
We crown you King of Kings and Lord of Lords;
There is none above your throne.
We lift you up with praises above;
You are our Messiah, the one we love.
We bow before you with humble hearts;
We cry out to you,
Our Lord Most High.
For our sins, you came and died;
Praises will forever be on our lips—
Hosanna! Hosanna!
For you we live.
We give you all honor and glory;
Our lips will forever tell the story.
You are Alpha and Omega,
The beginning and the end.
You reign and rule with your mighty hands;
You have all power and might.
You rule and reign with power and glory;
Our lips will forever tell the story.

The Overflow Blessing

I walk in the overflow blessing.
I didn't earn it; the blessing was earned on Calvary.
The blessing of the Lord makes you rich and adds
no sorrow with it.
The blessing can't be bought, sought, or caught;
It is freely given.
Accept Jesus Christ, God's only begotten son,
and then your journey has begun.
You are blessed in the city and in the field;
You are blessed in spite of how you feel.
Feelings come and go,
But blessings are always moving
Keep the current flowing;
Be a blessing to others.
Give, and it shall be given unto you;
Press down, shaken together, and running over.
The blessing is not just for you four and no more;
The blessing is like a river flowing.
All areas will be affected;
Nothing remains untouched.
I am blessed to be a blessing.

Let Down Your Net

Let down your net for a catch;
Your inheritance is waiting for you to possess it.
God has planned great things for his children;
You are a child of God.
God has not changed his mind;
God wants his children to be blessed beyond measure.
It is the will of God for us to increase in all areas.
Just as the disciples let down their nets and got
a boatload of fishes,
We are to let down our nets to receive our blessings.
Our future is bright in God's mind.
Eyes have not seen,
Ears have not heard
what God has for his people.
We are blessed in the city and blessed in the field;
Whatever we put our hands to will be blessed.
The blessing is before us, not behind us.
Favor opens the door;
Grace and mercy will propel you forward.
Open your mouth and call forth the blessing;
Let us go forth and possess the land.

Pregnant with Expectancy

I am pregnant with faith.
Faith comes by hearing, and hearing by the Word of God.
The Word of God is powerful.
The Word of God is full of power and anointing.
The seed of the Word is planted in my heart.
I water the seed with the Word and with prayer.
The seed of faith has been planted, watered, and attended to.
The seed is alive and growing strong.
The seed will produce thirty-, sixty-, and a hundredfold.
I am about to give birth to overflow blessings.
The blessings of the Lord make you rich and add no sorrow.
Faith moves like a current; it flows where the demand is placed on it.
Faith is flowing like a river into all areas of my life.

Bountiful Harvest

This is the time;
This is the season.
My harvest is due now;
This is my reaping season.
The harvest is plenteous;
The laborers are few.
I'm reaping above and beyond;
I have sown in abundance.
Seeds have been sown in good soil;
I water my harvest with joyful expectancy.
I have given thanks for my harvest;
Lack is broken over my life now.
The abundance of rain is falling;
The flow of increase is in my life.
The crop is ready and ripe for harvest;
This is the season to reap and not faint.
The best is yet to come.

I Get Up

I've been down, around, and almost to the ground,
But I get up.
I've been in the outhouse, the big house, and the White House,
But I get up.
I've been through depression, oppression, and recession,
But I get up.
I've been through storms, hurricanes, and all kinds of weather,
But I get up.
I've been to colored only, the back door, the side door, and the front door,
But I get up.
I've been through segregation, separation, and integration,
But I get up.
I've had no opportunity, fair opportunity, and equal opportunity,
But I get up.
I've been called no class, low class, and middle class,
But I get up.
I've had no pay, low pay, and minimum pay,
But I get up.
I've had no fan, a window fan, and an air conditioner,
But I get up.
I've had no car, a car, and a dream car,
But I get up.
I've been through sickness, troubles, and the deaths of loved ones,
But I get up.
I've had strife, sleepless nights, and offenses,
But I get up.
I've had no hope, some hope, and great hope,
But I get up.
I've been called gal, darkie, nigger, colored, black, and

African American,
But I get up.
I've been on the north side, east side, west side, and the south side,
But I get up.
I was a slave to sin; now I walk in the marvelous light.
I've had a sinful life, and now a blessed life.
I've had no expectations, some expectations, and great expectations,
Because Jesus was crucified on Calvary cross, and Jesus Christ got up;
Because the blood of Jesus covered my sins and yours;
Because Jesus has brought us a mighty long way;
Because we are free at last, free at last—
Thank God Almighty, we are free at last—
I get up!

Printed in the United States
By Bookmasters